Endangered Species

ISSUES

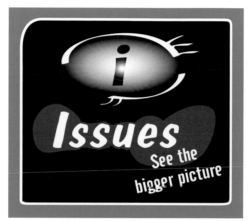

Volume 193

Series Editor

Lisa Firth

Independence

Educational Publishers

Cambridge

First published by Independence

The Studio, High Green

Great Shelford

Cambridge CB22 5EG

England

© Independence 2010

Copyright

Photocopy licence

British Library Cataloguing in Publication Data

Endangered species. -- (Issues ; v. 193)

1. Endangered species. 2. Nature conservation.

3. Biodiversity.

I. Series II. Firth, Lisa.

578.6'8-dc22

ISBN-13: 978 1 86168 544 5

Printed in Great Britain

MWL Print Group Ltd

CONTENTS

Chapter 1 The International Situation

Endangered species	1
Shocking global facts	3
Why does biodiversity matter to me?	6
100 questions to conserve global biodiversity	7
Biodiversity and Oil Palm project	8
Boosting biodiversity can boost global economy	10
UN report warns of economic impact of biodiversity loss	13
Brazil cattle giants unite to end Amazon destruction	14
Billion hectares of land have potential for forest restoration, study shows	15
Wildlife – cause for concern	16
Canned hunting	17
Year of the tiger	18
Elephants under threat	19
How the pet trade's greed is emptying south-east Asia's forests	20
World's most endangered primates revealed	22
What is the bushmeat trade?	23
Galápagos	24
Why we need to conserve invertebrates	26
£10m initiative to tackle bee and pollinator decline	27
Whales and dolphins in hot water	29
Ocean acidification	30
Consumer ignorance over endangered fish	30

Chapter 2 The UK Situation

Lost life: England's lost and threatened species	31
Bears, lynx, wolves and elk considered for reintroduction into British countryside	33
London's priority species	35
Fears grow for future of Britain's rarest butterflies	36
Red squirrel threats	37
Controlling non-native wildlife	38
Wildlife crime unit	39
Key Facts	40
Glossary	41
Index	42
Additional Resources	43
Acknowledgements	44

OTHER TITLES IN THE ISSUES SERIES

For more on these titles, visit: www.independence.co.uk

Alternative Therapies ISBN 978 1 86168 276 5
Food and Nutrition ISBN 978 1 86168 289 5
Energy Matters ISBN 978 1 86168 305 2
Exploited Children ISBN 978 1 86168 313 7
Stress and Anxiety ISBN 978 1 86168 314 4
Focus on Sport ISBN 978 1 86168 351 9
Transport Trends ISBN 978 1 86168 352 6
The Censorship Debate ISBN 978 1 86168 354 0
Gambling Trends ISBN 978 1 86168 375 5
Customers and Consumerism ISBN 978 1 86168 386 1
Coping with Disability ISBN 978 1 86168 387 8
Self-Harm ISBN 978 1 86168 388 5
A Genetically Modified Future? ISBN 978 1 86168 390 8
The Education Problem ISBN 978 1 86168 391 5
Vegetarian and Vegan Diets ISBN 978 1 86168 406 6
Mental Health and Wellbeing ISBN 978 1 86168 407 3
Media Issues ISBN 978 1 86168 408 0
Problem Drinking ISBN 978 1 86168 409 7
The Cloning Debate ISBN 978 1 86168 410 3
Sustainability and Environment ISBN 978 1 86168 419 6
The Terrorism Problem ISBN 978 1 86168 420 2
Religious Beliefs ISBN 978 1 86168 421 9
A Classless Society? ISBN 978 1 86168 422 6
Migration and Population ISBN 978 1 86168 423 3
Climate Change ISBN 978 1 86168 424 0
Euthanasia and the Right to Die
ISBN 978 1 86168 439 4
Sexual Orientation and Society
ISBN 978 1 86168 440 0
The Gender Gap ISBN 978 1 86168 441 7
Domestic Abuse ISBN 978 1 86168 442 4
Travel and Tourism ISBN 978 1 86168 443 1
The Problem of Globalisation
ISBN 978 1 86168 444 8
The Internet Revolution ISBN 978 1 86168 451 6
An Ageing Population ISBN 978 1 86168 452 3
Poverty and Exclusion ISBN 978 1 86168 453 0
Waste Issues ISBN 978 1 86168 454 7
Staying Fit ISBN 978 1 86168 455 4
Drugs in the UK ISBN 978 1 86168 456 1
The AIDS Crisis ISBN 978 1 86168 468 4
Bullying Issues ISBN 978 1 86168 469 1
Marriage and Cohabitation ISBN 978 1 86168 470 7
Our Human Rights ISBN 978 1 86168 471 4
Privacy and Surveillance ISBN 978 1 86168 472 1
The Animal Rights Debate ISBN 978 1 86168 473 8
Body Image and Self-Esteem ISBN 978 1 86168 484 4
Abortion – Rights and Ethics ISBN 978 1 86168 485 1
Racial and Ethnic Discrimination ISBN 978 1 86168 486 8
Sexual Health ISBN 978 1 86168 487 5

Selling Sex ISBN 978 1 86168 488 2
Citizenship and Participation ISBN 978 1 86168 489 9
Health Issues for Young People ISBN 978 1 86168 500 1
Crime in the UK ISBN 978 1 86168 501 8
Reproductive Ethics ISBN 978 1 86168 502 5
Tackling Child Abuse ISBN 978 1 86168 503 2
Money and Finances ISBN 978 1 86168 504 9
The Housing Issue ISBN 978 1 86168 505 6
Teenage Conceptions ISBN 978 1 86168 523 0
Work and Employment ISBN 978 1 86168 524 7
Understanding Eating Disorders ISBN 978 1 86168 525 4
Student Matters ISBN 978 1 86168 526 1
Cannabis Use ISBN 978 1 86168 527 8
Health and the State ISBN 978 1 86168 528 5
Tobacco and Health ISBN 978 1 86168 539 1
The Homeless Population ISBN 978 1 86168 540 7
Coping with Depression ISBN 978 1 86168 541 4
The Changing Family ISBN 978 1 86168 542 1
Bereavement and Grief ISBN 978 1 86168 543 8
Endangered Species ISBN 978 1 86168 544 5

EXPLORING THE ISSUES

Photocopiable study guides to accompany the above publications. Each four-page A4 guide provides a variety of discussion points and other activities to suit a wide range of ability levels and interests.

A note on critical evaluation

Because the information reprinted here is from a number of different sources, readers should bear in mind the origin of the text and whether the source is likely to have a particular bias when presenting information (just as they would if undertaking their own research). It is hoped that, as you read about the many aspects of the issues explored in this book, you will critically evaluate the information presented. It is important that you decide whether you are being presented with facts or opinions. Does the writer give a biased or an unbiased report? If an opinion is being expressed, do you agree with the writer?

Endangered Species offers a useful starting point for those who need convenient access to information about the many issues involved. However, it is only a starting point. Following each article is a URL to the relevant organisation's website, which you may wish to visit for further information.

Endangered species

It is estimated that there could be as many as 14 million species of plants and animals in the world, although only around two million have been officially recorded so far. More than 12,000 species of animals and plants now face extinction, due largely to human activities. Some will die out before they have even been discovered. Why are so many animals in danger?

Habitat destruction

Tropical rainforests are the world's richest natural habitats, housing more than two-thirds of all plant and animal species on Earth. Sadly, the rainforests are being destroyed at an alarming rate – with more than half already gone – for timber, and cleared so that the land can be used to graze farmed animals or to provide housing for expanding human populations. If rainforests disappear, all the plants and animals living there will be lost forever.

Six species of great ape who live in the tropical rainforests – the eastern and western gorilla, chimpanzee, bonobo, Sumatran and Bornean orang-utan – now face extinction. This is due to habitat destruction, and hunting.

Pandas live in the bamboo forests of China, another habitat that is being destroyed to make way for a rapidly growing human population. The panda population has been reduced to 1,500.

Hunting and trapping

People kill animals for their fur (to make coats and rugs), for their bones and horn (to make medicine or ornaments), for their flesh, and, sometimes, sadly, simply for the fun of it. Many animals are also trapped in the wild to supply the pet trade, or for use in circuses, zoos and aquaria. Others – in particular, primates – are captured and sold to research laboratories to be used in experiments.

The tiger is just one of many species of wild cat now facing extinction because of hunting and habitat loss. At the beginning of the 20th century, there were more than 100,000 tigers. Today, it is estimated that between 5,000 and 7,000 tigers remain in the wild. Three of the eight sub-species (the Bali, Caspian and Javanese) are already extinct. In the past, tigers were hunted for their skins (to make coats and rugs) and for sport. Today, tigers are still being killed for traditional Asian medicine. Virtually all of their body parts, including bones, eyes and whiskers, are used. Many Asian countries have recently signed up to the conservation agreement known as CITES and have agreed to ban the trade in tiger parts. Enforcing the law, however, is difficult and costly, while the profits made from the illegal trade are so great that some people feel it is worth the risk.

Whales have been ruthlessly hunted for centuries and, as a result, several species – including the giant blue whale – have been driven to the brink of extinction. This prompted the International Whaling Commission (IWC) to impose a moratorium (ban) on all commercial whaling in 1985. Norway, Japan and Iceland have continued to kill some species of whales.

Rhinos have roamed the earth for more than 40 million years, but after only a few centuries of intensive hunting they are now severely threatened. The world population of all five species is fewer than 15,000 animals. Rhinos are killed for their horn, which is ground up and used in traditional Asian medicine. This slaughter continues despite a CITES ban on the trade.

African elephants, the world's largest land animals, have also suffered a catastrophic decline. A century ago there were ten million animals, 20 years ago there were one million, but today there are only about 300,000 African elephants left. Most were killed for their ivory tusks, which are made into trivial trinkets and jewellery. In 1990, CITES banned the sale and trade in ivory and other elephant products but many elephants are still illegally shot by poachers.

Pollution

Rivers, seas and lakes are being poisoned with sewage, oil and toxic chemicals from industry. Human refuse also pollutes the environment and kills wildlife. Crops are sprayed with chemicals to kill bugs and insects, which in turn harm the animals who feed on them. Global warming and climate change caused by, amongst other factors, air pollution, also threatens lots of species with extinction.

In 2004, researchers identified 146 dead zones around the world's coastlines, areas where the dissolved oxygen levels are so low that no marine life can be sustained.

The animals who live in the oceans, particularly those at the top of the food chain, absorb these poisonous chemicals (including pesticides and industrial waste). For example, the bodies of seals, whales and dolphins and even Arctic polar bears have been found to contain high levels of toxic chemicals, which damage their ability to reproduce.

Why does it matter?

Some people say that we should conserve animals and plants because they might be useful to us in the future. It is also argued that, in the long term, our own survival may depend on maintaining the planet's ecosystems. This means preserving other species and maintaining the planet's biodiversity – or variety of life.

Animal Aid believe quite simply that we have a responsibility to protect animals for their own sake and especially those species which are at risk because of our actions.

Solutions

⇨ Conserve the world's natural habitats. Keeping alive endangered species in zoos is not a solution, because it becomes enormously difficult and expensive to repatriate them to their natural habitat. If we carry on polluting and destroying these habitats, repatriation becomes literally impossible. Only through protection of their habitats will wild animals survive.

⇨ Ban the international trade in products made from endangered species and enforce the laws that already exist to protect wildlife.

⇨ Educate people to help stop the trade in animal products.

⇨ Stop polluting the environment with poisonous wastes.

CITES (The Convention on International Trade in Endangered Species)

CITES is a United Nations agreement that protects endangered species by regulating or banning their trade. Unfortunately, not all countries belong to CITES, and enforcement efforts vary among those that have signed up. Even when someone is prosecuted, the punishments are usually trivial – ranging from minimal fines to short jail sentences, and are therefore little deterrent. Wildlife trafficking is one of the major forms of smuggling in the world, along with drugs and weapons.

What you can do!

⇨ Educate others about the plight of endangered species, and, if you go abroad, don't buy products made from them.

⇨ Contact the British Trust for Conservation Volunteers (www.btcv.org) and help manage local nature reserves.

A century ago there were ten million animals, 20 years ago there were one million, but today there are only about 300,000 African elephants left

⇨ Write to your MP (to find your MP, visit www.locata. co.uk/commons) and ask them to support legislation to protect natural habitats.

⇨ Avoid polluting packaging, and don't buy products made from tropical hardwood. Always look for the 'FSC' symbol to ensure that wood is from a sustainable source.

⇨ Join Animal Aid's youth group Youth4animals, and help campaign to save endangered species.

⇨ The above information is reprinted with kind permission from Animal Aid. Visit www.animalaid.org. uk for more information.

© Animal Aid

Shocking global facts

Information from the David Shepherd Wildlife Foundation.

Global wipe-out

An accelerating decline in species has led some experts to predict that the Earth is on the verge of a mass extinction – this one will be the first global wipe-out, caused by another species, with humans the dominant agent of destruction!

The Earth's resources

The Earth's supply of natural resources may only be able to sustain two billion humans by 2100 – not good news for a global population that currently stands at 6.4 billion and is expected to reach 8.9 by 2050, by which time the population in the 50 poorest countries will have tripled in size. Half a billion people already live in countries that are water-scarce and this is expected to triple in the next 20 years.

Growing population

In 1998, about 137 million humans were born and some 53 million died. This net gain of 84 million represents more than 230,000 additional residents reliant on the Earth's resources every day of the year – can our fragile planet survive?

Human consumption

Some experts predict that, with current trends, in 50 years time human beings will consume twice as many resources than the planet can replace every year.

Births in Africa

Every two weeks, more human babies are born in Africa than the number of elephants remaining in the wild on the entire African continent.

> *An accelerating decline in species has led some experts to predict that the Earth is on the verge of a mass extinction*

Acceleration

It took the entire history of human life until 1830 to reach a world population of one billion people. Now we are adding one billion people a decade to our current world population of over six billion.

One minute ago

Earth is 46 hundred million years old. Scale this down to 46 years, then modern man has been around for four hours and the Industrial Revolution began one minute ago. During those seconds, man has multiplied his numbers to plague proportions, ransacked the planet for fuels and raw materials and caused the extinction of countless species.

Consumption across the world

On average, every minute of the day, 274 people are born and 97 die. 177 extra people every minute means 93 million people each year. The vast majority of them are in third world countries that are least equipped to manage such growth. In ecological terms, it is not the simple population statistics that count, but the number of people multiplied by their average age consumption of energy and resources. The average US citizen consumes at least 50 times as much as the average Kenyan.

Cars in China

China reportedly has one million car owners. In ten years, this figure is estimated to rise to a staggering 200 million.

DAVID SHEPHERD WILDLIFE FOUNDATION

The top 300

The top 300 multinational corporations own 25% of the world's production resources. Incomes of the top ten surpass the collective gross national product of 100 of the world's smallest nations.

Profits

The world's wealthiest 200 companies saw their profits grow by 362.4% between 1984 and 2004. Their collective sales are now higher than the combined gross domestic product of all but ten nations on Earth. Since the top four US oil companies recently merged, their profits have soared by 146% – during what we were told was an 'energy crisis'.

First vs Third

5% of the world's population use up to 25% of the entire planet's energy resources and the wealthier 16% (mostly the US, Europe and Japan) use up to 80% of the world's goods. Yet, as you read this, 1.3 billion people can't even have a glass of clean water.

95% of all animals and plants that have ever lived on Earth have now become extinct

Logging in the Congo

Reports regarding a German company with a logging concession of one million hectares in central Congo have uncovered their 'sideline' of making shotguns for illegal hunters and transporting ammunition to the hunters in their company boats and aircraft. Observers saw and filmed seven smoked carcasses of endangered bonobos, a chimpanzee sub-species, killed for bush meat. Bonobo orphans are taken on company boats for sale in Kinshasa. Reports from hunters in four areas confirm that when the company camps move almost no wildlife remains. Enquiries show the company logs areas illegally while issuing 'ursprungzeugnis', which is an ex-Environment Minister's 'certificate', stating company operations are 'lawful and sustainable'.

Caviar

It is believed that the Russian mafia control 90% of the illegal trade in caviar, which can fetch up to £3,000 per kilo. One year, Customs seized 530kg of smuggled caviar at Heathrow alone.

Tropical timber

The world's $100 billion timber industry is running out of control, helped by the global market and fuelled by greed. Deforestation is wiping out plants and animal species, increasing soil erosion and flooding and contributing to 'global' warming. Commercial logging is believed to be responsible for the extinction of tens of thousands of species each year in tropical forests alone.

Extinction

95% of all animals and plants that have ever lived on Earth have now become extinct.

Tourism

Every tourist entering South Africa creates seven new jobs.

The Congo River

The Congo River descends from a plateau at about 1,000 feet high, through narrow canyons and 32 cataracts, to sea level in just 220 miles. The drop and volume of the water is so great that over the 220-mile descent it creates as much hydroelectric potential as all the lakes and rivers in the US.

Forest protection

A unique satellite-based survey of the planet's remaining closed forests, including virgin, old growth and naturally-regenerated woodlands, has found that over 80% are located in just 15 countries. The survey reveals that a surprising 88% are sparsely populated, for example the pressure from human population growth is low in Bolivia and Peru whilst in India and China the forests require urgent protection efforts.

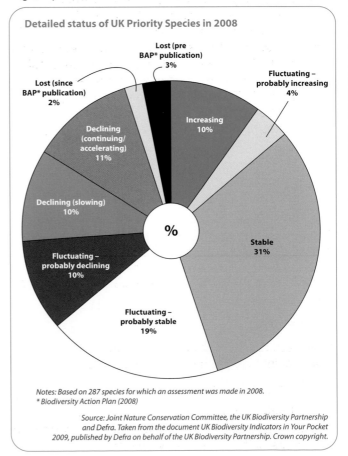

Detailed status of UK Priority Species in 2008

- Lost (pre BAP* publication) 3%
- Lost (since BAP* publication) 2%
- Fluctuating – probably increasing 4%
- Declining (continuing/accelerating) 11%
- Increasing 10%
- Declining (slowing) 10%
- Stable 31%
- Fluctuating – probably declining 10%
- Fluctuating – probably stable 19%

%

Notes: Based on 287 species for which an assessment was made in 2008.
* Biodiversity Action Plan (2008)

Source: Joint Nature Conservation Committee, the UK Biodiversity Partnership and Defra. Taken from the document UK Biodiversity Indicators in Your Pocket 2009, published by Defra on behalf of the UK Biodiversity Partnership. Crown copyright.

DAVID SHEPHERD WILDLIFE FOUNDATION

Turning the sea red

In 2001, staff at the Kazanli Soda-Chromium Factory in southern Turkey bulldozed the containing wall of an effluent-collecting basin, releasing its contents directly into the sea, turning it red and wiping out marine life with its highly toxic chemical discharge. This was particularly disastrous for turtles, since Kazanli's beaches host one of only three nesting populations in Turkey of the critically endangered Mediterranean green turtle.

70% of the Earth is covered by water but less than 25% is freshwater. Only 0.25% of this freshwater is actually accessible, with the rest stored deep underground or in ice

Litter

Approximately 6.5 million tonnes of litter finds its way into the world's oceans each year.

Phytoplankton

Studies have indicated that increasing ultra violet radiation (UVR) has limited the production of phytoplankton, the bottom of the food chain, by up to 23%, which may have catastrophic consequences for species within the ecosystem. After months of winter darkness, the first shafts of light signal the start of the Antarctic spring. Single-celled phytoplankton bloom underneath the melting ice floes. They are the basis of the marine food web and especially vulnerable to the effects of UVR. These 'floating gardens' supply the food for 500–700 million tonnes of krill which feeds at least 120 species of fish, 80 species of seabirds, six species of seals and 15 species of whale.

Destruction of the planet

Hard wood

Buy hard wood garden furniture in a British high street and you could be acquiring your own limited edition souvenir of Cambodia's disappearing rainforest. There is a deliberate attempt to use false labels to dupe unwary customers.

Ozone layer

Latest estimates indicate that the hole in the ozone layer is approximately 9.2 million square miles.

Rainforest

Brazil holds about one-third of the world's remaining rainforest. Between 2000 and 2005 nearly 35,000 square kilometres of the rainforest were lost.

England to Indonesia

On average you would probably find ten species of tree in a hectare of English woodland. In the same area in an Indonesian forest, there would be over 250 tree species.

Freshwater

70% of the Earth is covered by water but less than 25% is freshwater. Only 0.25% of this freshwater is actually accessible, with the rest stored deep underground or in ice. Much of this accessible water is stored in wetlands and yet over 50% of these areas have been destroyed in the last 100 years.

Climate

Climate change

Climate change is the greatest environmental threat the world currently faces. Extreme weather disasters are at an all-time high, with 16 recorded in the 1960s and 70 during the 1990s, and with the early part of the 21st century showing an even greater number of disasters. Today there is clear water at the North Pole in place of pack ice and carbon dioxide levels in the atmosphere are higher now than at any time in the previous 20 million years.

The USA

With less than 5% of the world's human population, the United States consumes 25% of the world's resources and is responsible for 25% of global greenhouse gas emissions. President Barack Obama is attending Copenhagen Climate talks in December 2009 and has pledged to reduce greenhouse gas emissions.

With less than 5% of the world's human population, the United States consumes 25% of the world's resources

Coral Reef

A comprehensive study on coral reefs, which support over 60% of the world's fish stocks and in fact occupy a much smaller area of the planet than previously thought (about half the size of France), warns that many of these ecosytems face extinction because of rising sea temperatures and human pressures.

⇨ The above information is reprinted with kind permission from the David Shepherd Wildlife Foundation. Visit www.davidshepherd.org for more information.

© David Shepherd Wildlife Foundation

DAVID SHEPHERD WILDLIFE FOUNDATION

Why does biodiversity matter to me?

Information from CBD-UN International Year of Biodiversity.

You are biodiversity. Most of the oxygen you breathe comes from plankton in the oceans of the world and lush forests around the globe.

The fruit and vegetables you eat were likely to have been pollinated by bees, and the water you drink is part of a huge global cycle involving you, clouds, rainfall, glaciers, rivers and oceans. Your diet depends almost entirely on the plants and animals around us, from the grasses that give us rice and wheat, to the fish and meat from both wild and farmed landscapes.

Your body contains up to 100 trillion cells and is connected with everything around you and the wider world in a wonderfully complex and timeless system. You share your atoms with every being and object in the natural world, you are both ancient and inconceivably young.

You share the planet with as many as 13 million different living species including plants, animals and bacteria, only 1.75 million of which have been named and recorded

Biodiversity is life, your life is biodiversity and biodiversity is you.

You share the planet with as many as 13 million different living species including plants, animals and bacteria, only 1.75 million of which have been named and recorded. This incredible natural wealth is a priceless treasure that forms the ultimate foundation of your human well-being.

The systems and processes these millions of neighbours collectively provide produce your food, water and the air you breathe – the basic fundamentals of life. As if that was not enough they also supply you with timber and plant materials for furniture, building and fuel, the mechanisms that regulate your climate, control floods and recycle your waste and the novel compounds and chemicals from which medicines are made. You may take biodiversity so much for granted, that it is sometimes easy to forget it's there – that you are a part of it and can't live apart from it.

Biodiversity's contribution to your life is not just practical, physical and utilitarian, it is also cultural. The diversity of the natural world has been a constant source of inspiration throughout human history, influencing traditions, the way our society has evolved and supplying the basic goods and services upon which trade and the economy is built. The disappearance of unique species is a loss that cannot be calculated and leaves us all much poorer.

The loss of iconic and symbolic species is not only a cultural tragedy, it also undermines our own survival. The beautiful, bountiful diversity of the natural world is being damaged as a result of human activities. Felling or burning of forests, removal of mangroves, intensive farming, pollution stress, overfishing and the impacts of climate change are all destroying biodiversity. We can stop this loss, the question is – will we?

The International Year of Biodiversity 2010 is our chance to prove we will.

⇨ The above information is reprinted with kind permission from CBD-UN International Year of Biodiversity. Visit www.biodiversityislife.net for more.

© CBD-UN International Year of Biodiversity www.biodiversityislife.net

100 questions to conserve global biodiversity

Conservation experts have identified 100 key scientific questions that, if answered, could help conserve global biodiversity.

Conservation experts from 24 world-leading organisations including the WWF, Conservation International and Birdlife International have identified 100 key scientific questions that, if answered, would help conserve global biodiversity. Scientists say if the questions are answered swiftly, it could stem massive biodiversity loss.

Some of the questions include: 'are there critical thresholds at which loss of biodiversity disrupts ecosystem functions and services?' and 'how effective are different methods for assessing ecosystem services?' The conservationists are also keen to find out how nanotechnology impacts on biodiversity. Other contentious topics – such as how ocean acidification might shape marine biodiversity and the effects of the changing water cycle on biodiversity – are also on the list.

> **'With the current crisis in the loss of habitats and species it is important that we ensure we are carrying out the most important research'**

According to the International Union for Conservation of Nature (IUCN), loss of biodiversity is accelerating despite a global convention committing governments to halt the decline. Experts say species and habitats are disappearing so fast there needs to be more effort focused on research that helps scientists understand what's behind the loss.

But there is a problem for conservation bodies trying to curb biodiversity loss. Sometimes, there is a mismatch between the conservation topics academics study and the information conservationists need to help them preserve biodiversity. The 100 questions, published online this week in the journal *Conservation Biology*, could help address this issue.

'With the current crisis in the loss of habitats and species it is important that we ensure we are carrying out the most important research,' says Professor William Sutherland of the University of Cambridge, lead author of the study and Miriam Rothschild Chair in Conservation Biology. 'When research is designed to meet the needs of real natural resource protection projects, it can lead to substantial gains for biodiversity,' he adds.

To address the mismatch, 761 conservationists from 24 of the world's leading conservation bodies and 12 academics generated a preliminary list of 2,291 questions relevant to conserving global biodiversity.

The group of experts used email voting to short-list the 2,291 questions before a smaller group of 44 met for two days at the University of Cambridge to decide on the final 100 questions. The questions are not ranked.

Before a question could be included in the 100, it had to meet eight strict criteria, including: it had to be answerable through realistic research; it had to address important gaps in knowledge; and it had to be on a time and space scale that could be addressed by a research team.

The resulting questions are divided up into 12 key sections reflecting issues the conservationists are worried about, such as 'climate change', 'ecosystem management and restoration', 'impacts of conservation interventions' and 'ecosystem function and services'.

Many of the 100 questions are at the heart of the biodiversity theme in NERC's strategy: *Next Generation Science for Planet Earth, 2007–2012*. The main overarching challenge within the theme is to understand the role of biodiversity in key ecosystem processes. Specific goals include: understanding which biodiversity thresholds will ultimately lead to extinctions and ecosystem change; understanding the impact of biodiversity loss on health; and developing new methods to assess the direct and indirect value of biodiversity to society.

The list of 100 questions builds on a hugely successful exercise conducted in 2008 to identify the top 25 emerging threats to biodiversity in the UK – also led by Professor Sutherland – widely used by researchers, funders and NGOs to direct their own research agendas.

The research was funded by the Natural Environment Research Council and the Department for Environment, Food and Rural Affairs.

22 April 2009

⇨ The above information is reprinted with kind permission from the Natural Environment Research Council. Visit www.nerc.ac.uk for more information.

© *Natural Environment Research Council*

NATURAL ENVIRONMENT RESEARCH COUNCIL

Biodiversity and Oil Palm project

Information from ZSL.

By Sarah Christie

Oil palm plantations are making a significant contribution to the ongoing disappearance of Indonesia's tropical forests and the unique assembly of species that call them home. However, the palm oil they produce is extremely profitable, meaning the stakes are high for both the industry and the diverse ecosystems that are under threat.

ZSL's Biodiversity and Oil Palm project will work with the palm oil industry to identify and implement practical measures that can be taken to reduce the impact it has on wildlife.

What is palm oil?

Whether you like it or not, you will probably have consumed a lot of palm oil in your lifetime. As the world's most popular vegetable oil, this versatile ingredient is hidden inside a huge number of the products you see on the supermarket shelf – from cereal bars and pizza to make-up and soap.

Often simply labelled as 'vegetable oil' on the label, a recent survey investigated just how many popular products contain palm oil. On top of this, the recent controversial craze for biofuel has increased demand even further.

Where does palm oil come from?

Brightly coloured fruits, which are rich in palm oil, grow on oil palm trees (*Elaeis guineensis*). Although oil palm is native to West Africa, the climate in Indonesia is perfect for growing this crop, making palm oil production a very lucrative business in Indonesia.

Consequently, oil palm plantations have expanded at a phenomenal pace over the past few decades, with the result that Indonesia recently became the biggest producer of palm oil in the world.

Oil palm plantations: death sentence or life line?

The debate surrounding the environmental and social impacts of the palm oil industry is an emotive but extremely complex one – it is impossible to label it as simply good or bad.

Whatever your viewpoint, there is little doubt that the expansion of oil palm plantations has played a leading role in the destruction of vast areas of rich tropical

> *Oil palm plantations are making a significant contribution to the ongoing disappearance of Indonesia's tropical forests*

forest in Indonesia, which has one of the highest rates of deforestation in the world.

This is of enormous conservation concern as these forests are home to an extraordinary variety of species, from the Sumatran tiger to the rhinoceros hornbill, many of which are totally unique to Indonesia.

Despite this, the palm oil industry makes a vital contribution to the Indonesian economy, generating nearly $8 billion worth of exports and providing over two million jobs, mainly in rural areas.

Abandoning palm oil production is not a viable option as it is one of the most productive and versatile vegetable oils available and the huge global demand for it provides a valuable revenue stream for Indonesia.

Although palm oil is important for the economy, expansion cannot continue if this is at the cost of Indonesia's natural ecosystems: the future of this country is highly dependent on the health of both.

The relationship between oil palm and biodiversity

Very little wildlife is able to live amongst the rows of oil palms, but previous ZSL research has shown that it is often a different story for the patches of damaged habitat and unplanted land that usually remain on an oil palm plantation.

This suggests that animals living in the surrounding forest, such as tapirs, tigers and clouded leopards, may use these patches of non-oil palm habitat to help them travel across the plantation to reach other areas of forest.

Since the expansion of oil palm plantations has both reduced the area of forest that remains and caused it to become fragmented, these connecting 'stepping stones' could provide a crucial lifeline to species whose future hangs in the balance.

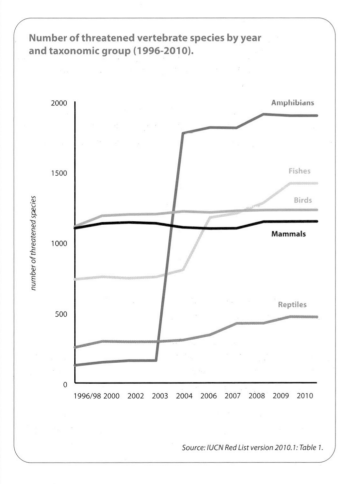

Number of threatened vertebrate species by year and taxonomic group (1996-2010).

Source: IUCN Red List version 2010.1: Table 1.

What is being done to readdress the balance?

The environmental damage caused by oil palm plantations has been widely publicised in recent years, creating an incentive for palm oil companies to improve their practice and an urgent need for practical guidance that will enable them to do so.

In response to this the Roundtable on Sustainable Palm Oil (RSPO) was established in 2004.

The RSPO provides a forum for discussion between concerned social and conservation NGOs and all sectors of the palm oil industry, aiming to promote a standard of palm oil production that respects people and the planet but still makes a profit.

Once a palm oil company has chosen to join the RSPO, they must satisfy various criteria before their palm oil can be certified as 'sustainable'.

This includes criteria which address the impact that oil palm plantations can have on the environment, right from pollution by pesticides to damage caused to wildlife and habitats that are a high priority for conservation.

In order to abide by the RSPO's criteria, palm oil companies must take steps to conserve areas with 'High Conservation Value' on their existing plantations and ensure that new developments do not damage any such areas.

For this to be possible, it is first necessary to identify exactly which areas are of 'High Conservation Value'.

At present, pin-pointing areas of habitat that are essential for the survival of the wide variety of species that may be present in the surrounding landscape and managing them effectively is proving extremely challenging.

Practical guidance that will enable companies to identify and manage areas of natural habitat that are a priority for conservation is urgently needed.

The aim of ZSL's Oil Palm and Biodiversity Project

ZSL has been awarded a grant from the Biodiversity and Agricultural Commodities Programme to work with the palm oil industry and the RSPO to develop an effective tool for assessing biodiversity in and around oil palm plantations that is compatible with the RSPO's Biodiversity Criteria.

Practical measures for managing the areas that support this biodiversity will also be tested, with regular biodiversity assessments used to determine how successful they are at improving the biodiversity value of the area they are implemented in.

Match funding for the project has been provided by the oil palm company Wilmar International, whose plantations (one in Kalimantan and one in Sumatra) will provide the focus for this research.

⇨ The above information is reprinted with kind permission from ZSL. Visit www.zsl.org for more.

© ZSL / Sarah Christie

Boosting biodiversity can boost global economy

2010 is litmus test of international community's resolve to conserve and enhance planet's natural assets.

A new and more intelligent pact between humanity and the Earth's economically-important life-support systems is urgently needed in 2010, the head of the UN Environment Programme (UNEP) said today.

Speaking at the launch of the UN's International Year of Biodiversity in Berlin today, UN Under-Secretary General and UNEP's Executive Director Achim Steiner said that an unprecedented scientific, economic, political and public awareness effort was needed to reverse – and to stop – the loss of the planet's natural assets.

These losses include its biodiversity such as animal and plant species and the planet's ecosystems and their multi-trillion dollar services arising from forests and freshwater to soils and coral reefs.

'The words biodiversity and ecosystems might seem abstract and remote to many people. But there is nothing abstract about their role in economies and in the lives of billions of people,' said Mr Steiner at the meeting hosted by German Chancellor Angela Merkel.

'Take coral reefs for example. The range of benefits generated by these ecosystems and the biodiversity underpinning them are all too often invisible and mainly undervalued by those in charge of national economies and international development support,' he added.

The latest estimates by The Economics of Ecosystems and Biodiversity (TEEB) study, which UNEP hosts, indicates that coral reefs generate annually up to US$189,000 per hectare in terms of coastal defenses and other areas of 'natural hazard management'.

'In terms of diving and other tourism revenues, the annual services generated equate to perhaps US$1 million; genetic materials and bio-prospecting, up to US$57,000 per hectare annually and fisheries, up to US$3,800 per hectare per year,' explained Mr Steiner.

Meanwhile, it is estimated, for example, that one-fifth of coral reefs are already seriously degraded or under imminent risk of collapse as a result of unsustainable human activities such as coastal developments, over-fishing, destructive fishing practices and pollution.

Climate change and ocean acidification, linked with the build-up of carbon dioxide, could eventually see 50 per cent and perhaps up to 100 per cent loss of coral reefs worldwide.

'If you factor the true value of coral reefs into economic planning, it is likely that far more rational and sustainable choices would be made in terms of development, emissions and pollution control and resource management. It is a similar story in respect to all of the planet's nature-based assets from forests and freshwaters to mountains and soils,' said Mr Steiner.

He added that 2010 was meant to be the year when the world reversed the rate of loss of biodiversity, but this had not happened.

> **'The words biodiversity and ecosystems might seem abstract and remote to many people. But there is nothing abstract about their role in economies and in the lives of billions of people'**

'I would urge heads of state here in Berlin and beyond to renew their commitment and set their sights broad and high. The urgency of the situation demands that as a global community we not only reverse the rate of loss, but that we stop the loss altogether and begin restoring the ecological infrastructure that has been damaged and degraded over the previous century or so,' stressed Mr Steiner.

He added that the International Year of Biodiversity would prove a success only if several litmus tests are met.

Science

There is an urgent need to bridge the gap between science and policy-makers in governments around the world.

In February, environment ministers attending UNEP's Governing Council/Global Ministerial Environment Forum will decide whether or not to establish an Intergovernmental Panel or Platform on Biodiversity and Ecosystem Services (IPBES).

UNITED NATIONS ENVIRONMENT PROGRAMME

'There is an urgent need to take forward the science, in part to sharpen our understanding of the natural world and unravel its complexities. For example, we still do not know how many species are needed within a given ecosystem to maintain its health and its economically-important services,' said Mr Steiner.

'There is also an urgent need to ensure that the wealth of science we already have is used by governments to maximum effect and genuine and sustained action on the ground,' he added.

The proposed IPBES is aimed at addressing these issues. Mr Steiner pointed out that governments should consider supporting the proposed new panel or give guidance on an alternative body or mechanism. He added the status quo was not an option if biodiversity loss is to be truly addressed.

Public awareness

Mobilising public support across countries, cities, companies and communities would be among the keys to a successful year.

'De-mystifying terms such as biodiversity and ecosystems and communicating complex concepts and sometimes obscure scientific terms, will also be vital to get people on board,' said UNEP's Executive Director.

'Linking livelihoods, the combating of poverty and the relationship between biodiversity and natural systems with the health of economies needs to set the tone. Equally the link between not only the threat from climate change but the role of living organisms and systems in buffering humanity against the worst impacts of global warming are messages that need to be heard loud and clear,' he added.

⇨ For example, an estimated five gigatonnes or 15 per cent of worldwide carbon dioxide emissions – the principal greenhouse gas – are absorbed or 'sequestrated' by forests every year, making them the 'mitigation engine' of the natural world.

⇨ Forests also capture and store rain-water, releasing it into river systems while also recycling a great deal of the nutrients upon which agriculture depends.

⇨ Marine ecosystems, including mangroves, salt marshes and sea-grasses are not only coastal defences and fish nurseries. It is estimated that they are absorbing and locking away greenhouse gases equal to half the world's transport emissions.

Economics

Bringing the economics of biodiversity and healthy ecosystems into mainstream economics and national accounts would be a major achievement.

TEEB, which builds on some 20 years of work, will publish its final report in advance of the tenth meeting of the Conference of the Parties to the Convention on Biological Diversity in Nagoya, Japan, in October this year.

However, its work so far has shed new light on how much the global economy is losing as a result of its failure to sustainably manage its natural capital.

⇨ The TEEB Interim Report estimated that annual losses as a result of deforestation and forest degradation alone may equate to losses of US$2 trillion to over US$4.5 trillion alone. The study is also underlining the huge economic returns from investing in nature.

⇨ It is estimated that for an annual investment of US$45 billion into protected areas alone, the delivery of ecosystem services worth some US$5 trillion a year could be secured. The study underlines that many countries are already factoring natural capital into some areas of economic and social life with important returns, but that this needs rapid and sustained scaling-up.

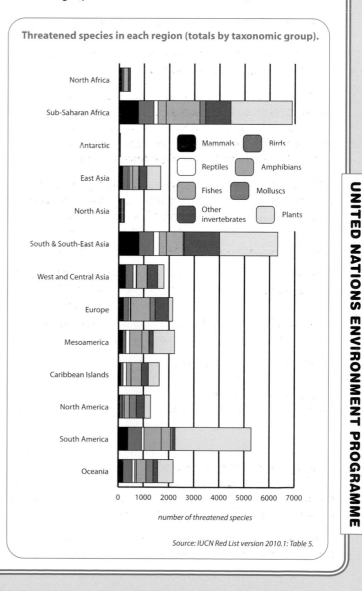

Threatened species in each region (totals by taxonomic group).

Legend: Mammals, Birds, Reptiles, Amphibians, Fishes, Molluscs, Other invertebrates, Plants

Regions (top to bottom): North Africa, Sub-Saharan Africa, Antarctic, East Asia, North Asia, South & South-East Asia, West and Central Asia, Europe, Mesoamerica, Caribbean Islands, North America, South America, Oceania

x-axis: 0, 1000, 2000, 3000, 4000, 5000, 6000, 7000

number of threatened species

Source: IUCN Red List version 2010.1: Table 5.

UNITED NATIONS ENVIRONMENT PROGRAMME

- ➪ In Venezuela, investment in the national protected area system is preventing sedimentation that otherwise could reduce farm earnings by around US$3.5 million a year.

- ➪ Planting and protecting nearly 12,000 hectares of mangroves in Vietnam costs just over US$1 million but saved annual expenditures on dyke maintenance of well over US$7 million.

- ➪ One in 40 jobs in Europe are now linked with the environment and ecosystem services ranging from clean tech 'eco-industries' to organic agriculture, sustainable forestry and eco-tourism.

'Among the positive outcomes of the recent UN climate convention meeting in Copenhagen was an agreement that Reduced Emissions from Deforestation and Forest Degradation (REDD) can join the existing options for combating climate change. In other words, paying developing nations to conserve forest systems so that the carbon remains locked in nature rather than emitted to the atmosphere,' said Mr. Steiner.

Other possibilities, ones that meet the climate but also the biodiversity challenge, could follow and should be taken forward in 2010.

These include carbon payments for farmers and landowners who manage agriculture and land in ways that reduce greenhouse gas emissions and enhance living systems and the role of marine ecosystems in climate including adaptation but also their importance in terms of biodiversity.

Alien invasive species

Part of the challenge that echoes the economic question includes addressing alien invasive species.

These are species that, as a result of international trade including shipping or deliberate introductions, can flourish unchecked in their new homes sometimes thousands of kilometres from where they are naturally found.

- ➪ By some estimates alien invasive species may be costing the global economy US$1.4 trillion or more while representing a further challenge to the poverty-related UN Millennium Development Goals.

- ➪ In sub-Saharan Africa, the invasive witchweed is responsible for annual maize losses amounting to US$7 billion: overall losses to aliens may amount to over US$12 billion in respect to Africa's eight principal crops.

'Improved international cooperation through the UNEP-linked Convention on Biological Diversity is needed and stepped up support for the Global Invasive Species Programme,' said UNEP's Executive Director.

'It is also important to boost the capacity of the responsible national customs and quarantine agencies, especially in developing countries and to accelerate controls on the movement of aliens via the UN's International Maritime Organization,' he added.

Access and benefit sharing

Successfully negotiating an international regime on access and benefit sharing of genetic resources at the CBD meeting in Japan would also be a landmark for 2010.

Currently, and in the absence of such a regime, many developing countries harbouring the richest source of genetic material are declining companies from developing countries and scientists access to these resources.

An international regime could foster cooperation and unlock the genetic resources available in the developing world for the development of new pharmaceuticals, new crop strains and materials for all nations.

In turn it could trigger financial flows from North to South and improve the economics of conserving biodiversity and ecosystems.

'Constructive negotiations are underway since the last meeting of the CBD in Bonn in 2008 and there is optimism that an international regime could be concluded to the benefit of developed and developing economies, to the benefit of biodiversity and ecosystems,' said Mr. Steiner.

Improved international environment governance

The international response to biodiversity loss and sustainable management of nature-based resources has been the establishment of several key bio-related treaties.

These include the CBD and its Cartagena Protocol on living modified organisms; the Convention on the International Trade in Endangered Species; the Convention on Migratory Species; the Ramsar Convention covering wetlands and the Africa Eurasia Waterbird Agreement.

Greater cooperation between the relevant treaties and agreements should be fostered in 2010 in order to accelerate the international response.

11 January 2010

- ➪ The above information is reprinted with kind permission from the United Nations Environment Programme. Visit www.unep.org for more information.

© United Nations Environment Programme

UN report warns of economic impact of biodiversity loss

The 'alarming' rate of nature loss could harm food sources and industry, and exacerbate climate change, UN report warns.

By Juliette Jowit

The 'alarming' rate at which species are being lost could have a severe effect on humanity, conservationists warned today. Targets set eight years ago by governments to reduce biodiversity loss by 2010 have not been met, experts confirmed at a UN meeting in Nairobi, Kenya.

The third *Global Biodiversity Outlook* report said loss of wildlife and habitats could harm food sources and industry, and exacerbate climate change through rising emissions.

The 'alarming' rate at which species are being lost could have a severe effect on humanity, conservationists warned today

Achim Steiner, the Executive Director of the United Nations Environment Programme (UNEP), said: 'Humanity has fabricated the illusion that somehow we can get by without biodiversity or that it is somehow peripheral to our contemporary world: the truth is we need it more than ever on a planet of six billion [people], heading to over nine billion by 2050. Business as usual is no longer an option if we are to avoid irreversible damage to the life-support systems of our planet.'

The report confirms what a coalition of 40 conservation organisations said last month, when they claimed there have been 'alarming biodiversity declines'. The coalition said that pressures on the natural world from development, over-use and pollution have risen since the ambition to reduce the rate of biodiversity loss was set out in the 2002 Convention on Biological Diversity (CBD).

The first formal assessment of the target, published at the end of April in the journal *Science*, is the basis of today's formal declaration. This week's meeting will see governments pressed to take the issues as seriously as climate change and the economic crisis.

'Since 1970 we have reduced animal populations by 30%, the area of mangroves and sea grasses by 20% and the coverage of living corals by 40%,' said Professor Joseph Alcamo, chief scientist of the UNEP.

'These losses are clearly unsustainable, since biodiversity makes a key contribution to human wellbeing and sustainable development.'

The *Science* study compiled 30 indicators of biodiversity, including changes in populations of species and their risk of extinction, the remaining areas of different habitats, and the composition of communities of plants and animals.

'Our analysis shows that governments have failed to deliver on the commitments they made in 2002: biodiversity is still being lost as fast as ever, and we have made little headway in reducing the pressures on species, habitats and ecosystems,' said Stuart Butchart, the paper's lead author.

'Our data shows that 2010 will not be the year that biodiversity loss was halted, but it needs to be the year in which we start taking the issue seriously and substantially increase our efforts to take care of what is left of our planet.'

The failure to meet the CBD target will not be a surprise to experts or policymakers, who have warned for years that too little progress was being made. Last month the head of the IUCN species survival commission, Simon Stuart, told the *Guardian* that for the first time since the dinosaurs, species were believed to be becoming extinct faster than new ones were evolving.

10 May 2010

Brazil cattle giants unite to end Amazon destruction

Information from Greenpeace.

At a signing ceremony in São Paulo today, four of the world's largest beef and leather companies agreed to ban the purchase of cattle from newly deforested land in the Amazon. The four – Marfrig, Bertin, JBS-Friboi and Minerva – dominate the world export market and supply the UK.

The move is due in part to pressure from British companies such as corned beef manufacturer Princes, which today announced its own support for the moratorium. Princes has joined Clarks, Adidas and Nike by announcing its determination to cancel contracts with suppliers unless their products are guaranteed to be free from Amazon destruction.

The report explains how cattle ranching is the leading cause of deforestation anywhere in the world

Reacting to the news, Greenpeace Executive Director John Sauven said:

'Today's announcement is a significant victory in the fight to protect the Amazon. Cattle ranching is the single biggest cause of deforestation globally, and the fact that these multibillion dollar companies have committed to cleaning up their supply chains will lead to real change in the Amazon.

'British companies have helped make this happen by getting tough with their suppliers, but this is not the end of the story. We now need to make sure that this agreement is properly enforced and extended to the entire cattle industry in Brazil.'

In June this year a Greenpeace report entitled *Slaughtering the Amazon* exposed the link between forest destruction and the expansion of cattle ranching in the Amazon. The report explains how cattle ranching is the leading cause of deforestation anywhere in the world.

The Brazilian cattle sector, which occupies 80 per cent of all deforested areas of the Amazon, is the country's most carbon-intensive industry. Brazil is the fourth largest source of greenhouse gas emissions in the world.

The event was attended by Governor Blairo Maggi of the Brazilian state of Mato Grosso, which has the highest rate of deforestation in the Amazon as well as the largest cattle herd in Brazil. Maggi announced that the state would support efforts to protect the Amazon and would provide high-resolution satellite images for monitoring.

Reacting to the news, a spokesperson from Princes said:

'Princes have held detailed discussions with our Brazilian suppliers regarding a moratorium on deforestation for cattle in the Amazon biome.

'Princes supports the need to bring about an industry-wide agreement to end deforestation and requires its suppliers in Brazil to operate in line with the principles outlined in Greenpeace's Commit or Cancel policy. We will continue to engage with our suppliers and NGOs to ensure that these conditions are being met.'

5 October 2009

⇨ The above information is reprinted with kind permission from Greenpeace. Visit www.greenpeace.org.uk for more information.

© Greenpeace

Billion hectares of land have potential for forest restoration, study shows

Land areas around the world totalling more than the size of Canada have been identified as having potential to be restored to good-quality, healthy forests, a new study has found.

As the global effort to help tackle climate change by reversing the Earth's alarming loss of forests steps up, scientists using sophisticated satellite mapping have produced a world map identifying areas in which more than a billion hectares of former forest land and degraded forest land has restoration potential.

> **'With a global population already approaching seven billion, and forecast to increase to more than eight billion by 2025, the pressure on all of our natural resources is immense'**

That's about six per cent of the planet's total land area, and restoring forests to some of these lands could be achieved without prejudicing other vital land uses, such as food production. The Global Partnership on Forest Landscape Restoration (GPFLR) also says that the needs and rights of indigenous peoples and others who depend on forests must be respected when considering restoration projects. GPFLR will now work with individual countries and local communities to deliver restoration where communities benefit.

'With a global population already approaching seven billion, and forecast to increase to more than eight billion by 2025, the pressure on all of our natural resources is immense,' says Tim Rollinson, Chairman of the GPFLR and Director-General of the British Forestry Commission. 'At the same time, the Earth's forests continue to shrink, and what's left is increasingly being degraded. We know how to restore forests and make them sustainable. We now also know where we should do it, so we should be getting on with it.'

The findings were announced today in London, England, at an international meeting of the GPFLR, of which the IUCN and the British Forestry Commission are founding members.

The assessment has revealed that the potential to restore the world's lost forests is much greater than the previous estimate of 850 million hectares. The GPFLR partners say that forest restoration can have a significant impact on climate change as well as improving lives, and that urgent action on restoration should be taken hand in hand with efforts to stop the continuing global loss and degradation of forests.

Preliminary analysis indicates that by 2030 the restoration of degraded forest lands could make the same contribution to the reduction of greenhouse gases as that which could be expected from avoided deforestation (70 Gt of CO_2 emissions), and perhaps as much as twice that amount. The GPFLR will work with countries over the next year to clarify and refine these figures on a country-by-country basis.

> **Preliminary analysis indicates that by 2030 the restoration of degraded forest lands could make the same contribution to the reduction of greenhouse gases as that which could be expected from avoided deforestation**

'Forest restoration experiences around the world provide evidence that, although it is impossible to replace a pristine forest once it's gone, many of the functions it originally provided can be restored,' says Stewart Maginnis, Director of the IUCN's Environment and Development Group. 'Forests provide such vital services, such as clean water and fresh air, that we can win on all fronts by bringing them back to life. We need to protect the forests we have left, and restore what we've lost.'

26 November 2009

⇨ The above information is reprinted with kind permission from the Forestry Commission. Visit www.forestry.gov.uk for more information.

© Forestry Commission

Wildlife – cause for concern

Ecosystems all over the world are now contaminated with a cocktail of man-made chemicals.

CHEM Trust is particularly worried about several potentially hazardous chemicals, especially those that are persistent, bioaccumulative or those which can disrupt hormones.

Persistent chemicals are those which don't break down easily in the environment, and which can therefore last for decades. A chemical is said to 'bioaccumulate' if it builds up in our bodies or in wildlife. Unfortunately, when a chemical is persistent and bioaccumulative (P&B) it may be passed from mother to baby via the egg, placenta or during suckling.

The hormone-disrupting chemicals are very worrying because even at extremely low doses they can disrupt the normal workings of the reproductive, immune, nervous and other hormonally controlled systems. They can do this by mimicking natural hormones or blocking their action, or altering the breakdown or synthesis of the body's own hormones. Sometimes these chemicals are also called endocrine-disrupting chemicals or EDCs for short, because it is the endocrine glands which secrete hormones.

Some pesticides and flame retardants are persistent, bioaccumulative or hormone disrupting. Similarly, chemicals with these worrisome properties may be found in many consumer products including certain stain repellents, cosmetics, personal care products and plastics.

Scientists have shown that many wildlife populations have already been affected by hormone disruptors

There is a growing body of scientific evidence on the adverse impacts of several man-made chemicals on wildlife species. Scientists have shown that many wildlife populations have already been affected by hormone disruptors. The impacts include:

⇨ thyroid dysfunction in birds and fish;

⇨ decreased fertility in birds, fish, shellfish and mammals;

⇨ decreased hatching success in birds, fish and turtles;

⇨ gross birth deformities in birds, fish and turtles;

⇨ metabolic abnormalities in birds, fish and mammals;

⇨ behavioural abnormalities in birds;

⇨ de-masculinisation and feminisation of male fish, birds and mammals;

⇨ de-feminisation and masculinisation of female fish and birds; and

⇨ compromised immune systems in birds and mammals.

The connection between effects in wildlife and the likely effects in humans are also being noted.

Day in, day out, terrestrial, freshwater and marine species are exposed to a toxic cocktail of many different man-made compounds and the concern is that such chemicals can undermine future generations of wildlife (and humans). There is not one ocean or continent from the tropics to the once-pristine polar regions that is not contaminated.

Ecosystems and wildlife everywhere including seals, whales, fish, polar bears, migratory birds and many other species have been seriously affected.

For example, research carried out on fish, in many UK estuaries indicates that there is significant feminisation of the males in these populations. The male fish should have sperm in their testes but many have egg material there instead.

> *Day in, day out, terrestrial, freshwater and marine species are exposed to a toxic cocktail of many different man-made compounds*

The researchers concluded that the chemicals responsible for these endocrine-disrupting effects come from sewage works and from industrial discharges.

Other interesting research has been carried out on the polar bears in northern Norway where 'pseudohermaphrodites' have been reported, and it seems that several females have a small penis.

More analysis of the data is needed, but toxic chemicals may pose a threat to the future of polar bears, particularly because many persistent chemicals undergo a process of global re-distillation and can be found at high levels in the polar regions. Furthermore, mammals that are top predators are exposed to particularly high levels via the food chain and in early life via the placenta and suckling.

CHEM Trust's most recent report is *Effects of Pollutants on the Reproductive Health of Male Vertebrate Wildlife – Males Under Threat* by Gwynne Lyons.

This report shows that male fish, amphibians, reptiles, birds and mammals have been harmed by chemicals in the environment. Widespread feminisation of male vertebrate wildlife is highlighted. These findings add to mounting worries about the role of hormone-disrupting or so-called 'gender-bending' chemicals in the environment, and the implications for human health.

⇨ The above information is reprinted with kind permission from CHEM Trust. Visit www.chemtrust.org.uk for more information.

© CHEM Trust

Canned hunting

The hunting of wild animals in a confined area from which they cannot escape is widely known as canned hunting. It is common in South Africa and North America and has become a massively lucrative industry.

Hunters are prepared to pay exorbitant fees to shoot an animal, often at close range, for a guaranteed trophy. The victims may be hand-reared and semi-tame. There are estimated to be more than 1,000 canned hunting operations in the USA alone,[1] while according to a recent report[2] nearly 54,000 animals were killed in 2004 in South African canned hunts. Hunters from Britain, the United States, Germany, Spain and France will pay many thousands of pounds to shoot a lion, leopard or other animal.

Canned hunting – what is it?

Canned hunting operations refer to the hunting of captive animals that are trapped within enclosures and have little chance of escape. Some canned hunt operations have recently begun to allow their clients to hunt these trapped animals remotely via the Internet.

The animals involved are often habituated to human contact, having been hand-raised and bottle fed, so are no longer naturally fearful of people. Such animals will approach people expecting to get fed – but instead receive a bullet. This makes it easier for clients to be guaranteed a trophy and thus the industry is lucrative and has expanded over time. The industry thrives in both North America and South Africa, although South Africa holds the unfortunate title of providing the most lion trophies from canned hunts.

Notes

1 Humane Society of the United States

2 Published by TRAFFIC

⇨ Information from the Born Free Foundation. Visit www.bornfree.org.uk for more information.

© Born Free Foundation

Year of the tiger

Big cats in big trouble.

WWF today outlined the current top ten trouble spots for tigers, in an interactive map that provides a unique overview of threats faced by wild tigers.

The interactive map has been released in advance of WWF's Year of the Tiger campaign, which launches on Sunday to coincide with the start of Chinese year of the tiger. The campaign aims to build critical momentum to ensure the protection of the species, working with world leaders towards the goal of doubling wild tiger numbers by 2022 – the next year of the tiger. A global tiger summit to be held in Russia in September, attended by Heads of Government from the tiger range countries, will be a focal point of the campaign.

'Since the last year of the tiger in 1998, tigers have lost 40 per cent of their habitat. They now occupy only seven per cent of their historic range,' said Diane Walkington, Head of Species at WWF-UK. 'Already, three tiger sub-species have gone extinct since the 1940s and a fourth one, the South China tiger, has not been seen in the wild in 25 years. WWF is committed to ensuring the remaining populations receive the protection they so desperately need.'

The global wild tiger population is believed to be as low as 3,200 at present, down from 100,000 at the start of the 20th century, and if left unchecked there is a chance that numbers will drop beyond a point of no return within many areas of Asia by 2022. WWF's map highlights the increasing threats faced by the species, including habitat loss, illegal trade and climate change.

The threats to wild tigers highlighted in the map include:

⇨ Pulp, paper, palm oil and rubber companies are devastating the forests of Indonesia and Malaysia, which are home to critical tiger populations;

⇨ Hundreds of new or proposed dams and roads in the Mekong region will fragment tiger habitats;

⇨ Illegal trafficking in tiger bones, skins and meat feeds continued demand in east and south-east Asia, and elsewhere;

⇨ More tigers are kept in captivity in the US state of Texas than are left in the wild – and there are few regulations to keep these tigers from ending up on the black market;

⇨ Poaching of tigers and their prey along with a major increase in logging is taking a heavy toll on Amur, or Siberian, tigers;

⇨ Tigers and humans are increasingly coming into conflict in India as tiger habitats shrink;

⇨ Climate change could reduce tiger habitat in Bangladesh's Sundarbans mangroves by 96 per cent.

'Tigers are being persecuted across the globe. They are being poisoned, trapped, snared, shot and squeezed out of their homes,' said Diane Walkington. 'But there is now real hope that this trend can be reversed. With 13 countries where wild tigers survive now pledging that they will work towards doubling wild tiger numbers by 2022, there has never been such an ambitious, high level of commitment from governments to work to save this iconic species.'

11 February 2010

⇨ By kind permission of WWF-UK. Source: www.wwf.org.uk/what_we_do/press_centre/?3702/, Jo Sargent, Senior Press Officer, WWF-UK, Year of the tiger – Big cats in trouble, 11 February 2010. Panda symbol © 1986 WWF World Wide Fund for Nature (formerly World Wildlife Fund ® WWF registered trademark.

© WWF-UK

Elephants under threat

For centuries, elephants have been exploited for ivory, as weapons of war, for ceremonial purposes, by the logging industry, and by zoos and circuses.

Population plummet

In the last century, elephant populations massively declined due to habitat destruction, increased agriculture and the bloody ivory trade. Rampant ivory poaching from 1979 to 1989 halved Africa's elephant population from 1.3 million to 600,000. Today numbers may be as low as 450,000.

Ivory ban enforced

After the 1989 ban, the price of ivory crashed and markets in Europe and the USA closed down. But some African countries called for a resumption of trade with Japan. In 1997, CITES[1] approved the sale of up to 60 tonnes of ivory from Botswana, Namibia and Zimbabwe to Japan. Elefriends predicted a rise in poaching.

Reopening trade

Poaching escalated and Born Free's evidence showed at least 6,000 elephants were killed and 17,000kg of illegal ivory was seized by customs in 1998–99. Born Free estimated this represented just 10–20% of the total slaughter. In 2000, CITES agreed 'no more trade', but in 2002 gave Botswana, Namibia and South Africa permission to sell a further 60 tonnes of ivory stockpiles to Japan. In 2004, a proposal to further relax current restrictions on trade was put forward.

In 2010 proposals by Tanzania and Zambia to transfer their elephant populations from Appendix I to Appendix II and for a one-off sale of over 100,000kg of ivory from government-owned stocks were defeated. However, poaching still continues.

Conservation status

Africa's elephants

1900 – 10 million

1979 – 1.3 million

1989 – 600,000

2007 – 400,000; IUCN2 status: 'Vulnerable'

Asia's elephants

1900 – 100,000

1995 – 50,000

2007 – 35,000; IUCN2 status: 'Endangered'

Notes

1   Convention on International Trade in Endangered Species

2   International Union for Conservation of Nature

⇨ Reproduced with permission from the Born Free Foundation. Visit www.bornfree.org.uk for more.

© Born Free Foundation

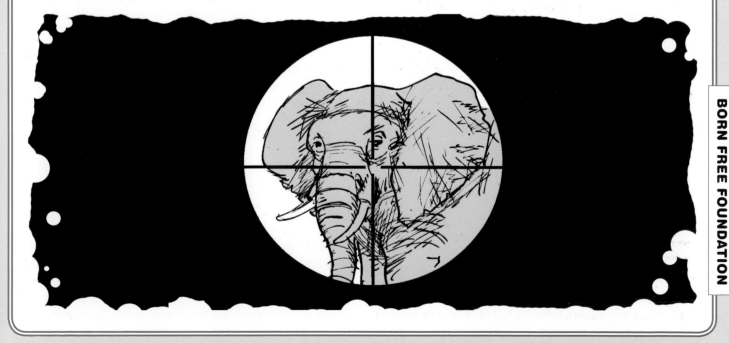

How the pet trade's greed is emptying south-east Asia's forests

Whole species disappear from the wild as millions of animals are illegally exported round the world in a business with profit margins that rival the drugs trade.

Countries across south-east Asia are being systematically drained of wildlife to meet a booming demand for exotic pets in Europe and Japan, and traditional medicine in China – posing a greater threat to many species than habitat loss or global warming.

More than 35 million animals were legally exported from the region over the past decade, official figures show, and hundreds of millions more could have been taken illegally. Almost half of those traded were seahorses and more than 17 million were reptiles. About one million birds and 400,000 mammals were traded, along with 18 million pieces of coral.

> *Countries across south-east Asia are being systematically drained of wildlife to meet a booming demand for exotic pets in Europe and Japan, and traditional medicine in China*

The situation is so serious that experts have invented a new term – empty forest syndrome – to describe the gaping holes in biodiversity left behind.

'There's lots of forest where there are just no big animals left,' says Chris Shepherd of Traffic, the wildlife trade monitoring network. 'There are some forests where you don't even hear birds.'

Seahorses, butterflies, turtles, lizards, snakes, macaques, birds and corals are among the most common species exported from countries such as Malaysia, Indonesia and Vietnam. Much of the business is controlled by criminal gangs, Shepherd says, and many of the animals end up in Europe as pets. The rarer the species, the greater the demand and the higher the price. Collectors will happily pay several thousand pounds for a single live turtle.

Vincent Nijman, a researcher at Oxford Brookes University who has investigated the trade, said: 'We see species that are in fashion traded in great numbers until they are wiped out and people can't get them any

more. So another one comes in, and then that is wiped out, and then another comes in.'

He added: 'In Asia, everybody knows the value of wildlife, so people go into the forest and, whatever they encounter, they know it has a value and that there is someone they can sell it to.'

Nijman's research offers the first glimpse of the size of this widespread trade. While most people are aware of illegal sales of rhino horn and ivory, he says it is the scale of the movement of lesser-known species that is most disturbing.

He analysed 53,000 records of imports and exports from countries under CITES, the international convention that regulates the sale of wildlife. Most common species are not listed under CITES, so do not appear in the records. Trade in the most endangered, such as rhino and

THE GUARDIAN

tiger, is banned. Nijman looked at species considered vulnerable enough that trade is allowed, but controlled. 'I'm not against the wildlife trade at all. I think it is a very important economic driver for a large part of the region and a lot of people are dependent on it,' he said. 'But it has to be done in such a way that you don't finish it all this year. It's not like oil, where you drill it out and then it's gone. If you organise and regulate it properly, it should go on for ever.'

CITES records between 1998 and 2007 showed that of more than 35 million animals exported during that period, some 30 million were taken from the wild. The EU and Japan were among the most significant importers.

For some mammal species, the proportion sourced from the wild dropped significantly over the decade, and traders were forced to rely increasingly on captive-bred animals. Official trade in birds virtually disappeared by 2007, probably because of bird flu restrictions.

The bulk of seahorses traded were in the form of dried specimens for Chinese medicine. 'The moment you look into the wildlife trade in south-east Asia, China is the biggest challenge, because they can use everything and they will use everything.'

Trade in the Asian pangolin, a scaly anteater, illustrates the problem. Officially, countries do not allow their commercial sale and agreed a zero quota under CITES in 2000, though regular seizures show widespread trade, for medicine and meat. 'The countries closest to China get emptied [of pangolin] first. Vietnam and Laos have been drained. Myanmar has been drained and they are working south, so now Indonesia is being emptied of pangolins,' Shepherd says. 'Prices are very high and in the next few years we will see pangolins being sucked out of Africa to supply the demand.'

Nijman says his analysis of the CITES records, published in the journal *Biodiversity and Conservation*, inevitably underestimates the scale of the trade. 'There is always an unknown quantity of CITES-listed species that are traded without being reported, and on top of that, probably much larger, is the trade in non-CITES species, which are the species that we think are still common enough to be traded without controls.'

One of these is the tokay gecko. 'Everyone who has been to Indonesia or Malaysia will know them because they are the ones that sit in your hotel room. You have them everywhere.' Although not listed by CITES, Indonesia has set a limit of 45,000 of the lizards exported each year as pets. Nijman says the true number traded is much higher, perhaps into the millions. 'We can't say whether a million tokay geckos being traded a year, or two million, is too many. Perhaps there are so many it is OK. But you would think that if they set the quota at 45,000 then a million is too much.'

Such geckos can be typically bought in rural villages for a few cents each, and sold for $10 – a profit margin that rivals the drugs trade. 'It's a great business. No wonder organised crime gets involved and starts running things,' Shepherd says. 'In Malaysia if you get caught selling drugs you get the death penalty. For wildlife crime the maximum fine is about $5,000.'

The situation is acute in south-east Asia, but the trade, both legal and illegal, is global, often using the Internet and courier delivery. For $4,000, an illegal trader based in Indonesia will send a three-year-old ploughshare tortoise – one of the most endangered animals in the world – from Madagascar.

Other species sell for as much as $20,000, though Nijman and Shepherd do not want to advertise which ones. 'People do know about the rhinos and the tigers, but the vast majority of this trade is in stuff that they didn't know existed,' said Shepherd. 'A handful of people are getting very rich and most people are getting screwed out of their natural resources.'

21 February 2010

© Guardian News and Media Limited 2010

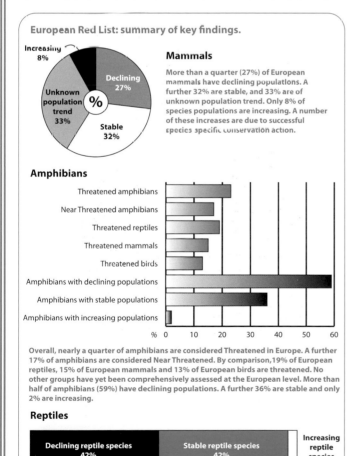

European Red List: summary of key findings.

Mammals

More than a quarter (27%) of European mammals have declining populations. A further 32% are stable, and 33% are of unknown population trend. Only 8% of species populations are increasing. A number of these increases are due to successful species specific conservation action.

Increasing 8%
Declining 27%
Unknown population trend 33%
Stable 32%

Amphibians

- Threatened amphibians
- Near Threatened amphibians
- Threatened reptiles
- Threatened mammals
- Threatened birds
- Amphibians with declining populations
- Amphibians with stable populations
- Amphibians with increasing populations

% 0 10 20 30 40 50 60

Overall, nearly a quarter of amphibians are considered Threatened in Europe. A further 17% of amphibians are considered Near Threatened. By comparison, 19% of European reptiles, 15% of European mammals and 13% of European birds are threatened. No other groups have yet been comprehensively assessed at the European level. More than half of amphibians (59%) have declining populations. A further 36% are stable and only 2% are increasing.

Reptiles

Declining reptile species 42%	Stable reptile species 42%	Increasing reptile species 3%

Overall, approximately one-fifth of reptiles are considered Threatened in Europe. A further 13% of reptiles are considered Near Threatened. By comparison, 23% of European amphibians, 15% of European mammals and 13% of European birds are Threatened. More than two-fifths (42%) of reptile species are declining and the same percentage is stable; only 3% are increasing.

Source: European Red List summary of key findings (extract). Directorate General for Environment, European Commission.

THE GUARDIAN

World's most endangered primates revealed

Mankind's closest living relatives – the world's apes, monkeys, lemurs and other primates – are on the brink of extinction and in need of urgent conservation measures according to Primates in Peril: The World's 25 Most Endangered Primates, 2008–2010.

The report, compiled by 85 experts from across the world, reveals that nearly half of all primate species are now in danger of becoming extinct from destruction of tropical forests, illegal wildlife trade and commercial bushmeat hunting. The list includes five primate species from Madagascar, six from Africa, 11 from Asia, and three from Central and South America, all of which are the most in need of urgent conservation action.

Conservationists want to highlight the plight of species such as the golden headed langur (*Trachypithecus p. poliocephalus*), which is found only on the island of Cat Ba in the Gulf of Tonkin, north-eastern Vietnam, where just 60 to 70 individuals remain. Similarly, there are thought to be less than 100 individual northern sportive lemurs (*Lepilemur septentrionalis*) left in Madagascar, and around 110 eastern black crested gibbons (*Nomascus nasutus*) in north-eastern Vietnam.

of primates for food, and the illegal wildlife trade. 'The results from the most recent IUCN assessment of the world's mammals indicate that primates are among the most endangered vertebrate groups,' says Dr Russell Mittermeier, Chair of the IUCN/SSC Primate Specialist Group and President of Conservation International. 'The purpose of our Top 25 list is to highlight those that are most at risk, to attract the attention of the public, to stimulate national governments to do more, and especially to find the resources to implement desperately needed conservation measures. We want governments to commit to desperately needed biodiversity conservation measures when they gather in Japan in October. We have the resources to address this crisis, but so far, we have failed to act.'

Despite the gloomy assessment, conservationists point to the success in helping targeted species recover. In Brazil,

Almost half (48 per cent) of the world's 634 primate species are classified as threatened with extinction

The list has been drawn up by primatologists working in the field who have first-hand knowledge of the causes of threats to primates. 'This report makes for very alarming reading and it underlines the extent of the danger facing many of the world's primates,' says report editor Dr Schwitzer, advisor to the IUCN/SSC Primate Specialist Group and Head of Research at the Bristol Conservation and Science Foundation. 'We hope it will be effective in drawing attention to the plight of each of the 25 species included. Support and action to help save these species is vital if we are to avoid losing these wonderful animals forever.'

Almost half (48 per cent) of the world's 634 primate species are classified as threatened with extinction on the IUCN Red List of Threatened Species™. The main threats are habitat destruction, particularly from the burning and clearing of tropical forests (which results in the release of around 16 per cent of the global greenhouse gases causing climate change), the hunting

the black lion tamarin (*Leontopithecus chrysopygus*) was down listed to Endangered from Critically Endangered on the IUCN Red List, as was the golden lion tamarin (*Leontopithecus rosalia*) in 2003, as a result of three decades of conservation efforts involving numerous institutions, many of which were zoos. Populations of both animals are now well-protected but remain very small, indicating an urgent need for reforestation to provide new habitat for their long-term survival.

The World's 25 Most Endangered Primates: 2008–2010, by region

Madagascar

⇨ Greater Bamboo Lemur *Prolemur simus*

⇨ Gray-headed Lemur *Eulemur cinereiceps*

⇨ Sclater's Black Lemur, Blue-Eyed Black Lemur *Eulemur flavifrons*

⇨ Northern Sportive Lemur *Lepilemur septentrionalis*

⇨ Silky Sifaka *Propithecus candidus*

Africa

⇨ Rondo Dwarf Galago *Galagoides rondoensis*

⇨ Roloway Guenon *Cercopithecus diana roloway*

⇨ Tana River Red Colobus *Procolobus rufomitratus*

⇨ Niger Delta Red Colobus Monkey *Procolobus epieni*

⇨ Kipunji *Rungwecebus kipunji*

⇨ Cross River Gorilla *Gorilla gorilla diehli*

Asia

⇨ Siau Island Tarsier *Tarsius tumpara*

⇨ Javan Slow Loris *Nycticebus javanicus*

⇨ Simakobu or Pig-Tailed Snub-Nose Langur *Simias concolor*

⇨ Delacour's Langur *Trachypithecus delacouri*

⇨ Golden-headed Langur or Cat Ba Langur *Trachypithecus p. poliocephalus*

⇨ Western Purple-faced Langur *Trachypithecus (Semnopithecus) vetulus nestor*

⇨ Grey-shanked Douc Monkey *Pygathrix cinerea*

⇨ Tonkin Snub-nosed Monkey *Rhinopithecus avunculus*

⇨ Eastern Black Crested Gibbon *Nomascus nasutus*

⇨ Western Hoolock Gibbon *Hoolock hoolock*

⇨ Sumatran Orangutan *Pongo abelii*

Central and South America

⇨ Cotton-top Tamarin *Saguinus oedipus*

⇨ Variegated or Brown Spider Monkey *Ateles hybridus*

⇨ Peruvian Yellow-tailed Woolly Monkey *Oreonax flavicauda*

⇨ The above information was co-written by Bristol Zoo, IUCN (the International Union for Conservation of Nature) and Conservation International. Visit www.www.bristolzoo.org.uk, www.iucn.org and www.conservation.org for more information.

© Bristol Zoo, IUCN and Conservation International

What is the bushmeat trade?

Information from the Born Free Foundation.

The killing of wild animals for their meat is known as the 'bushmeat trade'. In the past, bushmeat was largely a subsistence (hand to mouth) activity, and hunters took just enough to satisfy their families' needs. However, in recent years, it has become much more commercial. Increasing demand and profitability have meant bushmeat is supplied not only at the local level, but also for national and even international markets. To meet this growing demand, hunters are killing ever greater numbers of wildlife.

In Kenya, animals are hunted throughout the year and most are caught using indiscriminate snares. These snares are loops of wire which are set along the pathways that animals use to access feeding areas and water holes. As the animal walks along the pathway it may get its head or a limb caught in the snare. When the animal struggles, the wire snare tightens and the animal eventually dies a long and painful death.

Much of this hunting is illegal and the bushmeat trade is now threatening the survival of many wild animals. Indeed, the bushmeat trade is now the single biggest threat facing many wild animal species in Africa.

⇨ The above information is reprinted with kind permission from the Born Free Foundation. Visit www.bornfree.org.uk for more information.

© Born Free Foundation

Galápagos

The 'Rosetta Stone of Evolution' faces devastation from climate change and fishing.

The coastal wildlife of the Galápagos Islands – arguably the world's most celebrated environmental treasure – has suffered outright transformations due to a combination of climate change and overfishing, with several species of marine plants and animals believed to have gone extinct and many others seriously threatened, a new report reveals today.

The report, which is published today in the scientific journal *Global Change Biology*, outlines the massive impact that the increasing ocean temperatures associated with strong El Niño events have had on the archipelago which, coupled with fishing, tourism and other human activities, have changed Darwin's living laboratory forever.

> **Authors of the report believe that the Galápagos Islands are a 'canary in a coalmine' – a telling indicator of what the world has in store under global warming**

The report follows a major scientific meeting, convened by the Ecuadorian Ministry of Environment, the Galápagos National Park Service, Conservation International, WWF and other organisations, to assess the vulnerability of the Islands to climate change. Experts established that the El Niño weather cycle, possibly aggravated by global climate change and combined with other human impacts, has systematically impoverished the Galápagos marine environment in just a few decades.

Coral reefs and kelp beds have been eliminated, once-abundant marine species such as the Galápagos black-spotted damselfish (*Azurina eupalama*), Galápagos stringweed (*Bifurcaria galapagensis*), as well as the 24-rayed sunstar (*Heliaster solaris*) are thought to be extinct, and dozens of others – including the beloved Galapagos Penguin (*Spheniscus mendiculus*) – are within a hairsbreadth of annihilation. Based on the International Union for the Conservation of Nature Red List, two species are 'probably' extinct, another seven 'possibly' extinct, and a further 36 Vulnerable, Endangered or Critically Endangered. Climate change is predicted to make this devastating set of conditions more frequent and intense in the region.

On top of this, by comparing heavily to lightly fished areas in the Galápagos Marine Reserve, scientists learned that overfishing weakened the web of life in Galápagos through cascading effects of the expansion of sea urchin populations, which in turn erode its resilience.

The scientists that co-authored the report hope that the findings will demonstrate the urgency of taking action so that delegates at the international climate conference in Copenhagen later this month make tough commitments to adequately finance both measures to significantly reduce greenhouse gas emissions and to urgently address the climate adaptation needs of vulnerable communities and ecosystems.

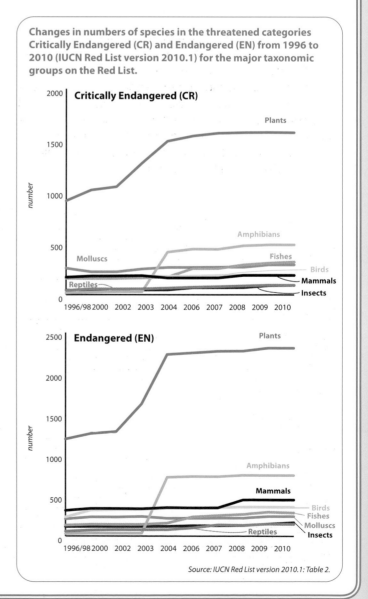

Changes in numbers of species in the threatened categories Critically Endangered (CR) and Endangered (EN) from 1996 to 2010 (IUCN Red List version 2010.1) for the major taxonomic groups on the Red List.

Source: IUCN Red List version 2010.1: Table 2.

Report coauthor Scott Henderson, Conservation International's Regional Marine Conservation Director in the Eastern Tropical Pacific, said: 'If marine species are going extinct in one of the most famous, and most cherished, World Heritage Sites, what is happening in the rest of the world that has been so little studied? It is time we recognise that the Ocean has limits just as the rainforests of the Amazon, the rivers of Europe, the ice sheets of the Arctic and the grasslands of the Great Plains. For seas to thrive we need increased efforts to slow climate change, more, bigger and better managed marine protected areas (MPAs) and better managed fishing activities outside MPAs.'

'The Galápagos, the Rosetta Stone of evolution, is now teaching us the far-reaching impacts of climate change on ocean ecosystems'

Authors of the report believe that the Galápagos Islands are a 'canary in a coalmine' – a telling indicator of what the world has in store under global warming. The archipelago lies at the convergence of several major ocean currents, which allows a diverse and unique set of ecosystems to co-exist – from penguins to marine iguanas to corals. However, during El Niño years, ocean temperatures throughout the Galápagos Marine Reserve rise a few degrees. These increases are roughly in line with those predicted under climate change scenarios for this region. During these years scientists are able to get a glimpse into the future of how wildlife and the people that depend on the environment might fare under climate change conditions.

Sylvia Earle, one of the paper's co-authors and one of the foremost authorities on marine issues, said: 'Nowhere on Earth are the combined impacts of climate change and overfishing more clearly defined than in the Galápagos Islands where unique assemblages of wildlife live on the sharp edge of change. Decades of data link recent fishing pressures to disruption of the islands' fine-tuned systems, making them more vulnerable to natural – and anthropogenic – changes in climate.'

Professor Les Kaufmann from Boston University said: 'The Galápagos, the Rosetta Stone of evolution, is now teaching us the far-reaching impacts of climate change on ocean ecosystems. Though too late to stop, we now know that the impacts of climate change can be softened by cutting back on fishing. The wildlife we eat today was part of the inner workings of an ecosystem which was under stress from global climate change and when these ecosystems are damaged, species and livelihoods can vanish in a heartbeat.'

4 December 2009

⇨ The above information is reprinted with kind permission from Conservation International. Visit www.conservation.org for more information.

© *Conservation International*

Numbers of Critically Endangered and Extinct mammal, bird and amphibian species occurring in and endemic to each of the 34 individual hotspots.

Hotspot	Critically Endangered mammals Occurring	Endemic	Extinct mammals	Critically Endangered birds Occurring	Endemic	Extinct birds	Critically Endangered amphibians Occurring	Endemic	Extinct amphibians
Atlantic Forest	7	5	0	15	11	0	4	4	1
California Floristic Province	2	2	0	3	2	2	0	0	0
Cape Floristic Region	2	1	1	0	0	0	3	2	0
Caribbean Islands	2	2	19	11	10	13	63	63	0
Caucasus	1	1	0	1	1	0	6	5	0
Cerrado	0	0	0	6	4	0	2	2	0
Chilean Winter Rainfall - Valdivian Forests	1	1	0	1	1	0	6	5	0
Coastal Forests of Eastern Africa	4	2	0	0	0	0	0	0	0
East Melanesian Islands	4	4	3	3	3	3	0	0	0
Eastern Afromontane	6	5	1	4	2	0	4	1	0
Guinean Forests of West Africa	6	6	0	4	4	0	11	9	0
Himalaya	3	2	0	4	1	0	0	0	0
Horn of Africa	5	3	1	4	3	0	0	0	0
Indo - Burma	12	9	1	7	3	0	2	2	0
Irano - Anatolian	0	0	0	0	0	0	0	0	0
Japan	3	3	3	2	2	4	2	2	0
Madagascar and the Indian Ocean Islands	12	12	3	12	12	32	9	9	0
Madrean Pine - Oak Woodlands	3	0	0	2	2	1	32	18	0
Maputaland - Pondoland - Albany	1	0	0	1	0	0	1	1	0
Mediterranean Basin	3	1	2	5	3	1	1	1	1
Mesoamerica	5	4	3	4	4	1	95	85	3
Mountains of Central Asia	2	0	0	0	0	0	0	0	0
Mountains of Southwest China	1	1	0	0	0	0	3	2	0
New Caledonia	0	0	0	3	3	1	0	0	0
New Zealand	0	0	2	7	7	20	1	1	0
Philippines	7	7	2	11	11	0	1	1	0
Polynesia - Micronesia	4	4	2	22	22	40	0	0	0
Southwest Australia	1	1	2	0	0	0	1	1	0
Succulent Karoo	2	0	1	0	0	0	0	0	0
Sundaland	14	12	2	9	7	2	4	4	0
Tropical Andes	6	3	0	15	14	0	115	103	2
Tumbes - Choc	2	1	2	6	5	2	7	1	0
Wallacea	1	1	3	7	7	0	0	0	0
Western Ghats and Sri Lanka	3	2	0	2	0	0	21	21	20

Source: Conservation International

CONSERVATION INTERNATIONAL

Why we need to conserve invertebrates

'If we and the rest of the back-boned animals were to disappear overnight, the rest of the world would get on pretty well. But if the invertebrates were to disappear, the world's ecosystems would collapse.' – Sir David Attenborough

At least 65% of all species on the planet are invertebrates. There are more than 32,000 terrestrial and freshwater and 7,000 marine species in the UK alone, and many are critically endangered.

If there are so many species, does it matter if some are lost? Yes, it does. They all have a critically important role to play in the web of life and they cannot be replaced once lost.

⇨ Invertebrates provide us with food and ecological, agricultural, medical and technological benefits.

⇨ Bugs are essential food to most birds and mammals.

Mankind has a responsibility to work within the environmental limits of the planet – otherwise we may be condemning many species, including ourselves, to extinction

⇨ Invertebrates are integral to ecosystem function – for instance, many of our wildflowers would be lost without insect pollination.

⇨ A lot of them may yet be recognised as of benefit to man, in areas such as biological pest control or medicine.

⇨ And most have incredible life stories yet to be told. We literally don't know what we are on the brink of missing.

Mankind has a responsibility to work within the environmental limits of the planet – otherwise we may be condemning many species, including ourselves, to extinction.

Just how threatened are invertebrates?

Habitat fragmentation, intense agricultural practices, climate change and many other human activities are damaging invertebrate populations.

One of the problems facing invertebrate conservationists is our lack of knowledge on their exact status. Perhaps this is unsurprising given that there are 40,000 species and only a few hundred experts who are studying them. However, what we do know presents a very worrying picture. Many species are in decline, and significant numbers of species are definitely or feared to be extinct.

⇨ Worldwide, an estimated 570,000 species could be extinct by 2100.

⇨ The *British Red Data Book for Insects*, published in 1987, includes 1,786 species whose continued existence is threatened – and that is just for the best-known groups.

⇨ Almost a third of all bees and wasps are under threat.

⇨ Over 70% of butterflies are declining significantly.

⇨ It is estimated that at least 15% of the total UK invertebrate fauna is under threat = 4,500 species in decline.

⇨ The Species of Conservation Concern list, which contains information on the designation and status of UK species, includes about 40% of the British fauna in well-known groups. If we extrapolate from this figure it would equate to 12,000 species of our land and freshwater invertebrate species.

⇨ Species such as the Short-haired bumblebee and the Essex emerald moth have become extinct in the last 15 years.

Invertebrates are integral to ecosystem function – for instance, many of our wildflowers would be lost without insect pollination

Most conservation organisations now recognise the problem but lack the information and expertise to integrate the conservation needs of such varied groups of animals.

There is clearly a great deal at stake and an enormous challenge to be met by Buglife.

⇨ Information from Buglife. Visit www.buglife.org.uk for more information.

© Buglife

£10m initiative to tackle bee and pollinator decline

Information from the Natural Environment Research Council.

Up to £10 million is to be invested to help to identify the main threats to bees and other insect pollinators under a major project announced today.

Pollinators – including honey and bumble bees, butterflies and moths – play an essential role in putting food on our tables through the pollination of many vital crops. These insects are susceptible to a variety of disease and environmental threats, some of which have increased significantly over the last five to ten years. Climate change, in particular warmer winters and wetter summers, has had a major impact on pollinators.

As a result, the numbers of pollinators have been declining steadily in recent years, with the number of bees in the UK alone falling by between ten and 15 per cent over the last two years.

> **Pollinators – including honey and bumble bees, butterflies and moths – play an essential role in putting food on our tables through the pollination of many vital crops**

To gain a better understanding of why this is happening, some of the UK's major research funders have joined together to launch an important new research programme.

The biggest challenge will be to develop a better understanding of the complex relationships between biological and environmental factors which affect the health and lifespan of pollinators.

The funding will be made available to research teams across the UK under the Living with Environmental Change (LWEC) partnership, the major initiative by UK funders to help the UK respond effectively to changes to our environment. This is a joint initiative from the Biotechnology and Biological Sciences Research Council (BBSRC), Defra, the Natural Environment Research Council (NERC), the Wellcome Trust and the Scottish Government.

Environment Secretary Hilary Benn:

'Aristotle identified bees as the most hard working of insects, and with one in three mouthfuls coming from insect-pollinated crops, we need to support bees and other pollinators.'

'I announced in January that Defra would put an extra £2 million into research funding, and I am delighted our partners have agreed to boost this to up to £10 million.'

'This funding will give some of Britain's world-class researchers the chance to identify the causes of the decline we're seeing in bee numbers, and that will help us to take the right action to help.'

Professor Douglas Kell, BBSRC Chief Executive:

'We are facing a fundamental problem with the decline of bees and other pollinators. They have an absolutely crucial role in pollinating many of our important crops. Without effective pollination we will face higher food

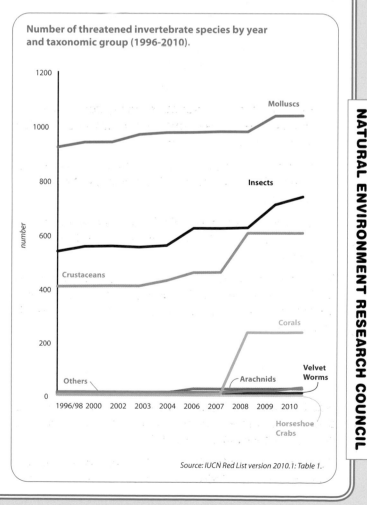

Number of threatened invertebrate species by year and taxonomic group (1996-2010).

Source: IUCN Red List version 2010.1: Table 1.

NATURAL ENVIRONMENT RESEARCH COUNCIL

costs and potential shortages. This programme will help us to understand why numbers have decreased and the steps we could take to reverse this. Complex problems such as this require a modern systems biology approach, a strategy at the core of BBSRC's vision. This will also feed into BBSRC's wider food security research programme which aims to deliver the science necessary to provide the nutritious and affordable food we need for the future.'

Professor Alan Thorpe, Chief Executive of NERC:

'Through the Pollinator Initiative, the LWEC partners will address what is a complex multidisciplinary problem. We need to conduct research that will help us to understand the links between bees and other pollinators and the range of environmental factors that affect them in various ways. This research will provide vital insights into why there has been a steep decline in these insect populations in recent years and help us to find solutions to the problem.'

'It is extremely important that we move swiftly to understand and try to reverse the decline in the populations of bees and other pollinating insects'

Sir Mark Walport, Director of the Wellcome Trust:

'It is extremely important that we move swiftly to understand and try to reverse the decline in the populations of bees and other pollinating insects. The devastating effect that this decline may have on our environment would almost certainly have a serious impact on our health and wellbeing. Without pollinating insects, many important crops and native plants would be severely harmed.'

Richard Lochhead, Cabinet Secretary of the Scottish Government:

'It is vital that we increase our understanding of the issues affecting populations of bees and other pollinators such as wasps, butterflies and beetles and in particular whether these are due to climate change. The impact these insects have on our rural industries, such as the soft fruit sector, and on plant biodiversity across Scotland cannot be under-estimated. Any reduction in numbers could have catastrophic consequences not just for our environment but also for our economy. I welcome this initiative and am confident the results of the programme will enhance our knowledge and help prevent further declines in bee numbers.'

Elin Jones, Minister for Rural Affairs of the Welsh Assembly Government:

'Honeybees and other pollinators are vital for local food production, which is the key to environmentally sustainable farming. By working with the other partners in this initiative, Defra have shown their commitment to safeguarding the population of the honeybee in the UK.'

The funding programme will be administered through BBSRC. The NERC Centre for Ecology and Hydrology will provide post-award coordination for the programme and contribute special expertise in long-term and large-scale ecology that will strengthen the research effort.

21 April 2009

⇨ The above information is reprinted with kind permission from the Natural Environment Research Council. Visit www.nerc.ac.uk for more information.

© *Natural Environment Research Council*

NATURAL ENVIRONMENT RESEARCH COUNCIL

Whales and dolphins in hot water

More whales, dolphins and porpoises than was previously thought could be at risk from the effects of climate change, according to a new study.

A University of Aberdeen scientist has found that climate change is likely to affect where 88% of the world's whale, dolphin and porpoise species – collectively known as cetaceans – are found.

Some species, such as the Common Dolphin and the Striped Dolphin, are likely to benefit from warming of the seas caused by climate change because areas of water suitable for them are expected to increase.

But for almost half of cetacean species, areas of suitable habitat are likely to shrink, and smaller areas of suitable habitat generally means fewer animals, says the study which appears in the journal *Endangered Species Research*.

For 21% of the world's 78 marine cetacean species this decline in habitat availability could be so dramatic that it will greatly increase the risk of extinction, the research has found.

While polar species such as the Narwhal and the Beluga are already known to be at risk from any reduction in suitable habitat, this study highlights for the first time that many species found in more temperate waters may also be in jeopardy.

Dr Colin MacLeod, a research fellow at the University of Aberdeen, conducted the study. He said: 'In the past, the main concern was for the small number of polar species likely to be affected by a decline in sea ice. However, this new study shows that there are many more species to be worried about.

'Some species found in temperate waters may be at risk not just because of the water temperatures they live in, but also because they only live in shallow waters. These species cannot simply respond to increases in sea temperature by moving into cooler neighbouring areas if the waters there are too deep.'

In Europe, the population of White-Beaked Dolphins found in the North Sea and nearby coastal areas are thought to be at greatest risk, according to the study. With no other large areas of suitable shallow habitat nearby, this population cannot simply move into cooler waters to the north as temperatures increase.

In the worst case scenario, according to the research, this could lead to a dramatic decline in their numbers and even the loss of the whole population if areas of suitable habitat disappear completely.

Further afield, a variety of temperate water species found in shallow waters around the coasts of South America, South Africa, Australia and New Zealand are also at high risk, the research found.

This includes an entire group of poorly-known dolphin species, those of the genus *Cephalorhynchus*, various porpoise species and southern hemisphere relatives of the White-Beaked Dolphin.

The study also raises concerns for the critically-endangered Vaquita, the world's smallest marine cetacean and one of the rarest, that is found only in the Gulf of California in Mexico. The enclosed nature of the Gulf of California may prevent this species moving into cooler waters as temperatures increase.

Even species whose habitat could expand may face other problems, according to the research. Moving into new areas could see cetaceans mixing with other species they normally don't mix with which could lead to them being exposed to new parasites and diseases to which they have little or no immunity.

Dr MacLeod also warns that expanded habitats could see species moving out of areas set up to protect them, potentially increasing their exposure to other human impacts such as bycatch in fisheries.

Understanding how the distribution of cetacean species is likely to be affected by climate change will need to become an increasingly important component of any conservation plans as waters warm, the study suggests.

Dr. MacLeod added: 'Without this understanding, we cannot plan for the future and we may be left simply watching species disappear from areas where they were once common as the full impacts of climate change start to bite.'

Future work planned by Dr MacLeod will use computer modelling to provide a more detailed picture of how different species are likely to react to future changes in climate. This will allow these changes to be taken into account when working out how best to conserve whales, dolphins and porpoises around the world now and in the future.

1 June 2009

⇨ The above information is reprinted with kind permission from University of Aberdeen. Visit www.abdn.ac.uk for more information.

© *University of Aberdeen*

UNIVERSITY OF ABERDEEN

Ocean acidification

News from Copenhagen.

Marine life in all the world's oceans is at risk due to rapidly increasing acidity of the sea caused by rising CO_2 levels, warn scientists on Oceans Day at the Copenhagen Climate Summit.

Although much of the world's oceans remain unexplored, severe marine ecosystem decline is predicted as a result of climate change and damage is already apparent in coral reefs.

Ocean acidification is being coined by many environmentalists as the 'evil twin' of climate change. Resulting from increased CO_2 levels in the atmosphere, ocean acidity has increased by 30% since the Industrial Revolution.

Increased ocean acidity is proven to limit the growth of key micro-organisms that sustain the marine food chain and biodiversity.

'Ocean acidification is a huge threat to global biodiversity, in particular coral reef systems, which support one quarter of all marine species', warned Ellycia Kolieb, a marine scientist from the environmental organisation Oceana.

To ensure the long-term viability of coral reefs, marine scientists are proposing reducing atmospheric CO_2 concentrations from today's level of 387 ppm to below 350 ppm.

The UK Secretary of State for Environment, Food and Rural Affairs, Hilary Benn MP, highlighted the limited attention ocean acidification receives compared to others being discussed by climate change negotiators.

A UK secondary school and the Plymouth Marine Laboratory have created an award-winning animation called *The Other CO_2 Problem* to highlight the issue of ocean acidification. The film, funded by the European Project on Ocean Acidification (EPOCA), was launched at the Copenhagen Climate Change Conference.

The predicted decline in marine ecosystems will have alarming consequences for coastal communities worldwide, including the loss of natural coastal defences, food insecurity, and declining commercial industries including fishing and tourism.

Ellycia Kolieb, involved in negotiations at the Copenhagen Climate Change Conference, states, 'it is essential that negotiators and political leaders understand the importance of the ocean to all of us'.

James Scipioni writes from Copenhagen where he is a British Council Climate Champion at COP15. James is part of the London 21 Sustainability Network who are an IYB-UK partner.
16 December 2009

⇨ Information from the NHM/IYB-UK. Visit www. biodiversityislife.net for more information.

Consumer ignorance over endangered fish

The British taste for fish and chips could be driving species to the edge of extinction, according to a new survey that found the majority of people do not even try to make sustainable choices about seafood. By Louise Gray, Environment Correspondent.

Fish stocks are down all over the world, with some species such as the bluefin tuna now considered to be as endangered as the white rhino and even the British favourite cod in danger of overfishing.

But a survey of more than 2,000 people found 78 per cent do not even try to buy fish from a sustainable source.

However, 70 per cent of consumers said they were more likely to make ethical choices when given the facts.

The survey comes as a new film by former *Daily Telegraph* journalist Charles Clover reveals the threat of overfishing to the oceans. *End of the Line*, to be released in cinemas on 8 June 2009, claims that seafood will be fished out by 2048 unless more is done to conserve stocks.

But the YouGov poll commissioned by Waitrose found more than half of people are unaware of the warnings fish stocks could be wiped out completely within this century if we continue as we are.

Mark Price, Waitrose Managing Director, said everyone should be asking where their fish comes from.

'The booming human population could wipe out fish stocks within this century if we don't act now. This is an environmental disaster and it will have a real and tangible impact on us all – as consumers, retailers, chefs or fishermen.'

2 June 2009

Lost life: England's lost and threatened species

Executive summary of a report from Natural England.

England is rich with life. Our diverse natural heritage includes myriad animals, plants and fungi. These species provide us with food and livelihoods; they help form the distinctive English landscapes and seascapes that we love; they have inspired and delighted through generations. They are England's life.

This life is being lost. Although changes in species populations are a natural consequence of environmental change, recent technological advances have led to humans altering species' habitats in ways and at rates that make it impossible for them to adapt. This has led to the decline and loss of many of England's native species, losses that matter both for the intrinsic value of the species themselves, and because they are associated with damage to our natural environment

Red squirrels have been lost from most counties in England while the purple emperor butterfly has been lost from the West Midlands and East of England regions

In this report, we highlight the fauna and flora for which England is special, and provide the first assessment of decline and loss across all types of species in England. We also identify those species at greatest risk of being lost next from England, should current trends continue. Finally, we describe the main actions that need to be taken to halt and then reverse the decline in these species. We have timed the release of the report to coincide with the United Nation's International Year of Biodiversity 2010 to help raise awareness of England's biodiversity and the fact that species are being lost from our own shores.

England has approximately 55,500 species of animals, plants and fungi. These include five groups of species considered to be of outstanding significance in an international context: Atlantic ferns, mosses and lichens; breeding seabirds; wintering and passage waterbirds and gulls; grassland and woodland fungi; and heathland invertebrates. We also have at least 40 species endemic to England (i.e. they occur nowhere else on Earth) and 54 species recognised as threatened at an international level.

We have been able to document the loss of 492 species from England, the vast majority of these being lost since 1800. This is likely to be a considerable underestimate of the true number of native species lost because relatively little is known about losses (or indeed the very existence) of species in the larger groups such as the many invertebrates, lower plants and fungi. The information on losses for the better studied groups reveal:

⇨ 24% of butterflies, 22% of amphibians, 15% of dolphins and whales, 14% of stoneworts, 12% of terrestrial mammals and 12% of stoneflies have been lost from England.

Some species that have been lost from England, such as the great auk and Ivell's sea anemone, are now globally extinct. The latter was lost from its last known site in the world, a brackish lagoon in West Sussex, as recently as the 1980s.

The principal agents of species loss and decline have been the destruction of natural habitats or their inappropriate management, and the persecution of wildlife that was considered a nuisance, a threat to livelihood or a prize specimen. Rates of loss have varied over time and between species groups. In invertebrates the rate of loss increased steadily during the 19th century to a peak in the first decade of the 20th century and has apparently since declined.

On a regional and local scale, the loss of species has been even more significant. Red squirrels have been lost from most counties in England while the purple emperor butterfly has been lost from the West Midlands and East of England regions. Some of the best data regarding local losses are from flowering plants. An assessment of loss from 23 English counties concluded

NATURAL ENGLAND

that, on average, one species of plant has been lost every two years at a county level since 1900. Rates of loss in southern and eastern counties have generally been highest.

As a result of these local and regional losses, a significant number of England's remaining species are under threat. A total of 943 English species were identified in 2008 as priorities for conservation action under the England Biodiversity Strategy and UK Biodiversity Action Plan (BAP). Further species have declined in recent historic times to precariously low ('depleted') levels. In the better known groups, the proportion of native species which appear on the BAP list or which have historically depleted populations represent:

⇨ all of the remaining reptiles, whales and dolphins, 57% of amphibians, 43% of freshwater fish, 37% of terrestrial mammals and seals, 35% of bumblebees and 33% of butterflies.

On average, 26% of England's species are depleted or on the BAP list.

Taking account of recent declines and emerging threats, in particular climate change, we have identified 12 groups of species that are of particular concern:

⇨ Species now severely restricted in range.

⇨ Internationally important wintering and passage waterbird populations.

⇨ Internationally important breeding seabird populations.

⇨ Species associated with coastal habitats.

⇨ Species losing their English 'climate space'.

⇨ Specialist farmland wildlife.

⇨ Long-distance migrants.

⇨ Predators exposed to illegal persecution.

⇨ Native species under pressure from invasive non-natives.

⇨ Amphibian species at risk from disease.

⇨ Marine fish at risk from overfishing.

⇨ Species exposed to nutrient enrichment.

Many of the species losses and declines that have occurred were avoidable. Whilst some of the species lost can never be brought back, there are reasons to be hopeful that we can reverse current trends in declining species. Some species that had been lost, such as the chough, have returned to England in recent years and have stayed in the much-improved habitat now available to them. We have also successfully re-introduced two species to England (red kite and large blue butterfly) and have re-introduction programmes underway for pool frog, corncrake, great bustard and interrupted

brome. Targeted conservation efforts have resulted in improving fortunes for many priority species on the original BAP list: 12% were reported as increasing in England in 2008, and a further 33% had stabilised. Nevertheless, the challenge ahead of us is significant, made all the more so by climate change, and we identify six priorities for action:

⇨ Better protect and manage the remaining wildlife habitats.

⇨ Restore and create additional high-value wildlife habitat including through enhancements at a landscape scale.

⇨ Establish a coherent network of Marine Protected Areas.

⇨ Establish more sustainable practices for all our land and seas.

⇨ Reduce the impact of invasive non-native species.

⇨ Take further steps to reduce illegal killing and collecting of our native species.

The fate of England's species is not only in the hands of Government or large landowners – we all have a role to play. Past losses and declines have been the consequence of the choices that we have made in the past. We now need to take responsibility and plan for the future. Our aim must be to restore a healthy natural environment with functioning ecological processes, in which species can thrive and reach new self-sustaining levels, for the benefit of us all. The time for action is now.

⇨ The above information is the executive summary of the report *Lost life: England's lost and threatened species* from Natural England, and is reproduced with permission. Visit www.naturalengland.com for more information.

© Natural England 2010

Bears, lynx, wolves and elk considered for reintroduction into British countryside

Lynx, brown bears, wolves and elk are among a range of animals being considered for reintroduction to the countryside centuries after they died out in Britain.

A report compiled for Britain's largest national park has identified 23 species of mammals, birds, amphibians and fish that once thrived in Britain and have the potential to live here again.

Ecologists who wrote the report, which is still in draft form, claim that large carnivores such as wolves, brown bears and the Eurasian lynx can all have beneficial impacts on the environment and act as a huge draw for tourism.

Campaigners have been pushing for lynx and wolves to be reintroduced in Britain as they could help control deer numbers and so protect woodland areas, which can be devastated by large herds.

Researchers claim it would require at least 250 brown bears and a similar number of wolves to maintain viable populations of the animals.

But the report warns that as a result such large species would be difficult to sustain in relatively small areas of land and can pose a threat to livestock unless carefully managed.

Proposals to reintroduce large carnivores into the wild have met with opposition from landowners and farmers while they have also sparked fears that the predators could pose a threat to humans.

The Cairngorms National Park report is due to be presented to the park's board later this year and will be used to help decide which species the park authorities will attempt to reintroduce into the Highlands.

Among the other species put forward as possible candidates in the report are large herbivores such as elk, typically found in Scandinavia, reindeer and the Eurasian beaver.

> **Campaigners have been pushing for lynx and wolves to be reintroduced in Britain as they could help control deer numbers and so protect woodland areas, which can be devastated by large herds**

Dr David Hetherington, an ecologist with Cairngorms National Park Authority and an expert on species reintroduction, insisted that some of the species such as common cranes, lynx and beavers were stronger candidates than others.

He said: 'We were trying to identify those animals we know or strongly suspect existed here in the past, in which human activity was a major factor in their decline or eventual extinction in this country.

'One animal that could be considered in the relative short term for reintroduction to this part of Scotland, however, would be the common crane, as it would have very little impact in terms of needing to be managed.

'Wolves are certainly viable but their introduction could create quite a few problems in the countryside. Out of all of the large carnivores we looked at, the Eurasian lynx is the best candidate and would have the best ecological impact.

NOW... WHERE WAS I...?

THE TELEGRAPH

'These are theoretical candidates for reintroduction, but the brown bear is not a species likely to be a realistic candidate for further consideration.'

European brown bears currently survive in parts of Eastern Europe, such as the Romanian forests, Russia and in parts of Scandinavia. Small populations also exist in the French Pyrenees, Italian Alps and in the Austrian Alps after reintroduction projects in the 1990s.

They are thought to have died out in Britain shortly before the medieval period due to heavy deforestation and hunting by humans.

Bones and skulls have been found scattered in many parts of the Scottish Highlands while bears are often depicted on Pictish stones.

The omnivores typically dwell in forests, feeding on berries, grasses, honey, insects, fish, carrion and small mammals.

While its American cousin is known to kill an average of two people every year, there have only been three fatalities due to brown bears in Scandinavia in the past century.

The report states that while brown bears would be a very significant wildlife tourism attraction and icon, the Highlands would struggle to support enough bears to produce a viable population.

Wolves are also known to have been present in Britain at least until the early 18th century, when they were eventually killed off through persecution by landowners and hunters.

The report claims that wolves, which are currently found in the US, Eastern Europe and parts of Scandinavia, could help to reduce grazing pressure on forestry by controlling deer numbers while also providing a significant tourism attraction.

The report also proposes introducing Western polecats, which were driven out of Britain by the late 19th century, and wild boar, which have been extinct in the UK for at least 300 years.

But it concludes that the Eurasian lynx, beaver and common crane are the most likely candidates for reintroduction due to successes elsewhere in Europe.

Lynx, which disappeared from the UK around 1,000 years ago, could be reintroduced using animals captured in continental Europe where there are now populations living in Germany, Switzerland, Poland, Slovakia and France following reintroductions.

The common, or Eurasian, crane is a large wetland bird thought to have become extinct in the 17th century.

There are already attempts to reintroduce the Eurasian beaver into the UK with a pilot scheme currently under way on the west coast of Scotland and there are plans to reintroduce the species in Wales.

Natural England conducted a feasibility study on the reintroduction of the beaver across the UK, finding that the animals could help to boost wildlife populations by creating new habitats and prevent flooding by slowing the flow of water with the dams they build around their burrows.

Areas that have been suggested as potential sites for beaver reintroduction include the Weald of Kent, the New Forest, Bodmin Moor and the Lake District. Landowners, however, claim beavers could destroy crops and damage woodland.

Species reintroduction has been a controversial subject in recent years and Natural England has faced intense criticism over proposals to reintroduce the white-tailed sea eagle.

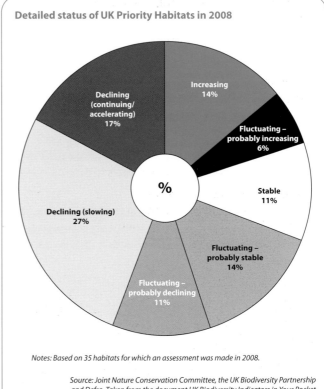

Detailed status of UK Priority Habitats in 2008

- Increasing 14%
- Fluctuating – probably increasing 6%
- Stable 11%
- Fluctuating – probably stable 14%
- Fluctuating – probably declining 11%
- Declining (slowing) 27%
- Declining (continuing/accelerating) 17%

Notes: Based on 35 habitats for which an assessment was made in 2008.

Source: Joint Nature Conservation Committee, the UK Biodiversity Partnership and Defra. Taken from the document UK Biodiversity Indicators in Your Pocket 2009, published by Defra on behalf of the UK Biodiversity Partnership. Crown copyright.

Ross Montague, director of the Scottish Countryside Alliance, a body who represent supporters of the countryside, said: 'Conservation efforts, in the Cairngorms and throughout Scotland, should be focused on maintaining and enhancing the native species already present – not introducing alien species which may or may not have been present in the dim and distant past.

'We are especially concerned with proposals to introduce species which could have unknown impacts on our fragile biodiversity and already endangered species such as the Scottish wildcat.'

27 February 2010

© Telegraph Media Group Limited 2010

THE TELEGRAPH

London's priority species

Information from London Wildlife Trust.

These are some of the rarer species that call London their home. All the species in this article are under threat and most are currently on the London Biodiversity Action Plan.

Bats

In Britain there are 16 species of bat, of which several can be found across London. Bats have been sighted in all the London boroughs and the small pipistrelle in particular maintains populations in the inner London boroughs.

Black redstart

With less than 100 pairs nesting in Britain, the black redstart is a rarer British breeding bird than the osprey or golden eagle. London is one of the UK's most important locations for this species.

Frogs and toads

The spread of London's urban environment has led to the destruction of the vast majority of the ponds that existed in the region. The survival of London's amphibians has been severely threatened by this loss.

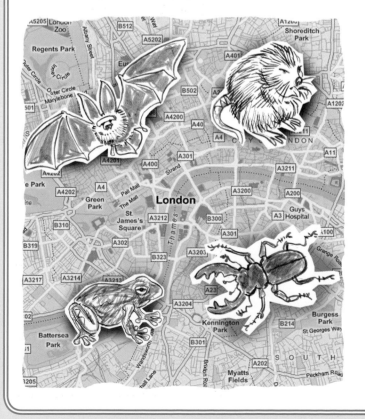

Hedgehog

Hedgehogs were long cited as an urban success story, but recent research points to an alarming decline in Britain's numbers. It appears that London's hedgehogs are disappearing, but the cause of this decline remains something of a mystery.

House sparrow

Once a common bird in London, the rate of decline of the cockney sparrow is truly alarming. House sparrow populations decreased in London by as much as 59 per cent in the seven years between 1994 and 2001 according to a national survey.

> ## In Britain there are 16 species of bat, of which several can be found across London

Peregrine falcon

The fastest bird in the world, peregrine falcons have been seen occasionally in and around London for many years, but since the late 1990s, peregrines have been a regular sight above the skies of the capital.

Stag beetle

The stag beetle is a globally threatened species but, perhaps surprisingly, London is nationally important for the population it supports. It is common in hotspots in south and west London.

Water vole

Britain's largest vole found fame in *The Wind in the Willlows*, but 'ratties' have declined at an alarming rate over the last 100 years. American mink has been largely responsible for its recent decline, although water voles do still thrive in some parts of the capital.

⇨ The above information is reprinted with kind permission from London Wildlife Trust. Visit www.wildlondon.org.uk for more information.

© London Wildlife Trust

Fears grow for future of Britain's rarest butterflies

Conservationists concerned as numbers continue to plummet.

Figures for butterfly sightings in 2009 have raised fears that five of Britain's rarest butterflies face a growing risk of extinction. Their numbers last year either continued to plummet or remained at near rock bottom levels.

Conservationists are particularly concerned about the Duke of Burgundy, which has reached new low points in each of the past three summers and is now at its lowest level since monitoring began. The butterfly, which 50 years ago was a common sight in woodland clearings, now has less than 80 colonies throughout the whole of the UK. Other rare butterflies that remained at very low levels in 2009 include the High Brown Fritillary, with less than 50 colonies, and the Wood White and the Lulworth Skipper, both of which are down to under 100 colonies. Another rare species, the Pearl-bordered Fritillary, had its second worst year in 2009.

Concern for the future of these butterflies follows analysis of data collected by the UK Butterfly Monitoring Scheme (UKBMS) from over 1,000 sites nationwide. The UKBMS is co-ordinated by the UK Centre for Ecology & Hydrology and the charity Butterfly Conservation.

Experts believe that the extremely wet weather throughout the summers of 2007 and 2008, followed by the above average rainfall of July and August 2009, have accelerated a long-term decline in numbers. Heavy rain makes it hard for butterflies to survive.

And it's not just the rare butterflies that are having a tough time. According to the new data, collected in the course of last year by the UKBMS, some relatively common species including the Wall Brown, Small Skipper and Green Hairstreak also remained at very low numbers in 2009. The Small Tortoiseshell, which has suffered a serious decline in recent years, made a slight comeback.

The highlight of 2009 was the massive migration of Painted Lady butterflies, which originated in North Africa and arrived in vast swarms in early summer. At one point it was estimated there could have been over a billion Painted Ladies in the UK. However, the UKBMS figures indicate that this migration was not quite on the scale of the last big one in 1996.

The UKBMS statistics show a very modest overall recovery compared with the dire summer of 2008, which was the worst for 25 years. In addition to the abundance of the Painted Lady, some native butterflies also did well in 2009. These included the Green-veined White, Ringlet and Speckled Wood – all of which thrive in lush woodland areas and may have been beneficiaries of the damp but not particularly cold conditions.

Dr Tom Brereton, Head of Monitoring with the charity Butterfly Conservation, said: 'We are particularly concerned about the Duke of Burgundy. At the start of the century there were about 200 colonies in the country. This number has now more than halved – and most colonies that remain are small. It is a serious situation.'

Butterflies are important as indicators, alerting us to underlying problems with the environment. If butterfly numbers are falling, inevitably other wildlife is in decline.

Figures for butterfly sightings in 2009 have raised fears that five of Britain's rarest butterflies face a growing risk of extinction

The main factors causing the long-term decline of many butterfly species include the loss of crucial habitats such as flower-rich grassland and the intensification of farming methods. A lack of management is also causing problems in habitats such as woodlands.

Each year the UKBMS collates data collected by hundreds of volunteers nationwide. Dr Marc Botham, a butterfly ecologist at the Centre for Ecology & Hydrology who analysed the results, said: 'The results show the enormous value of long-running datasets in identifying environmental problems. We are extremely grateful to the many volunteers who contribute each year. Through their efforts a new milestone was reached in 2009 when the number of sites monitored passed the 1,000 mark for the first time.'

5 March 2010

⇨ The above information is reprinted with kind permission from Butterfly Conservation. Visit www.butterfly-conservation.org for more information.

© Butterfly Conservation

Red squirrel threats

The red squirrel faces three main threats to its survival in Scotland today.

Threat 1: the spread of grey squirrels

The rapid spread of the North American grey squirrel in Britain is the main threat to red squirrel survival. The arrival of grey squirrels in an area occupied by red squirrels causes reduced red squirrel breeding and survival rates, leading to a gradual decline in their numbers.

The North American grey squirrel is an invasive non-native squirrel species introduced to Britain around the turn of the twentieth century. Compared with red squirrels, grey squirrels are more robust as a species. They are physically larger and, unlike red squirrels, can feed on seeds with high tannin content, such as acorns, thanks to differences in digestive physiology. As a result, more food sources are available to greys and they tend to put on 20% in body weight over autumn, compared with 10% for reds. This gives grey squirrels an advantage in hard winters. These differences allow grey squirrels to compete more successfully than red squirrels for food and habitat. In areas where red and grey squirrels exist together, the presence of grey squirrels results in reduced survival rates amongst red squirrel young and reduced reproductive rates, causing the gradual decline in red squirrel populations over time. This effect can already be seen in Scotland's central belt where grey squirrel spread has resulted in the almost complete disappearance of our native red squirrels.

Maps of red and grey squirrel distribution show how the spread of grey squirrels has resulted in the almost complete loss of red squirrels from England between 1940 and today, apart from remnant populations in northern England.

Maps of Scotland show how the spread of grey squirrels over the last ten years alone has significantly reduced red squirrel populations, particularly in central and south-western areas; continuation of this trend would threaten the survival of red squirrels in north Scotland.

While areas in north Scotland still remain grey squirrel free, Scotland is one of the only safe places left for red squirrels in Britain. Our red squirrels account for around 75% of the entire UK population. But grey squirrels are on the move! We must act now to protect our remaining red squirrels. If we do nothing, the red squirrel could become extinct on mainland Scotland.

Threat 2: squirrelpox

Grey squirrels can also bring another problem for red squirrels through the spread of the squirrelpox virus. This virus, carried by grey squirrels without causing them harm, is fatal to our native reds.

Often mistaken for myxomatosis, the virus lodges in red squirrels' eyelids and mucous membranes, which become infected and swollen, and produces scabs in and around the eyes, nose, mouth, feet, ears and genitalia. The infected squirrel is very quickly unable to see or to feed properly and rapidly becomes malnourished. The disease is highly infectious to red squirrels and kills within 15 days of infection. Although the means of transmission is still being investigated, it is possible that the virus could be transmitted by secretions left on feeders, dreys (the nest of a squirrel) or branches. Squirrelpox is already present in south Scotland as grey squirrels, some carrying squirrelpox, spread northwards from England. Red Squirrels in South Scotland (RSSS), the sister project of SSRS, is working to set up a pox-free buffer zone to contain the spread of the virus. For more information, visit the official RSSS website at www.red-squirrels.org.uk

Threat 3: habitat fragmentation

While grey squirrel spread is the main reason for the decline in red squirrel populations in Scotland today, habitat fragmentation is also a contributing factor.

Squirrel habitat fragmentation occurs when areas of woodland and forestry become segmented and separated by development and changing land-use. This leads to isolated areas which cannot sustain viable populations of wildlife, including red squirrels.

SSRS aims to directly address the factors contributing to red squirrel decline. This includes working with landowners to improve habitat conditions to help red squirrels thrive and increase in number as well as working to halt the decline of red squirrel populations in key areas of north Scotland through the prevention of further grey squirrel spread.

⇨ The above information is reprinted with kind permission from Saving Scotland's Red Squirrels (SSRS). Visit www. scottishsquirrels.org.uk for more information.

© Scottish Wildlife Trust

SAVING SCOTLAND'S RED SQUIRRELS

Controlling non-native wildlife

Plants and animals brought into the UK from abroad can cause great damage to native wildlife. Find out how you can help stop the spread of harmful species, and understand the laws on bringing plants and animals into the UK.

Why is non-native wildlife a threat?

Animals or plants have been brought to this country for hundreds of years. Most of them are not a problem. However, some plants and animals spread more aggressively, and can threaten native wildlife through competition, disease or by preying on them.

This can upset the balance of wildlife in this country. In extreme cases this could lead to some UK species disappearing for good.

Non-native plants and animals can cause financial harm to industries like forestry, agriculture and fisheries, and structural damage to buildings and roads. Floating pennywort, for example, grows very quickly and can cause damage to other plants and animals. Japanese knotweed can even grow through hard road surfaces, and once established is difficult and expensive to remove.

Examples of problem non-native wildlife

Being able to identify non-native wildlife could help you to stop the spread.

Floating pennywort

This is also called 'water pennywort' or sometimes just 'pennywort'. It has shiny, kidney-shaped leaves with crinkled edges and is usually found floating on still or slow-moving fresh water. Floating pennywort can grow up to 20 centimetres a day, blocking out light and reducing the oxygen for other plants and animals.

Japanese knotweed

Japanese knotweed is a fast-growing weed that appears to have no natural enemies in Britain. It spreads quickly and can damage property (for example by growing through tarmac or even the floors of houses). A fragment of root as small as 0.8 grams can grow to form a new plant.

American bullfrog

The American bullfrog eats almost any other species, and carries a disease that has wiped out many other frog and toad populations. It breeds rapidly, with each female laying up to 30,000 eggs at a time.

Grey squirrel

The grey squirrel has spread widely, with a population now estimated at over two million. They cause damage to woodland, and are largely responsible for the falling numbers of red squirrels in England. They are stronger and more adaptable than the red squirrel and they carry the squirrelpox virus, which is lethal to red squirrels.

A list of some of the key non-native species, descriptions and photographs can be found on the Non-Native Species website (www.nonnativespecies.org).

You can find more advice on dealing with invasive plants and harmful weeds in the 'Home and community' section (www.direct.gov.uk/en/HomeAndCommunity/InYourHome/PestAndWeedControl/DG_10037530).

How do non-native species arrive here?

Some non-native animals and plants are brought to this country deliberately. Sometimes they enter the country by accident – insects, small animals, seeds and plant fragments can be carried on luggage or as stowaways in cargos of internationally transported goods.

There are restrictions on the type and amount of plants that you can bring back from abroad. More details of these limits can be found in the *If in doubt, leave it out* leaflet from the Department for Environment, Food and Rural Affairs (Defra) – www.defra.gov.uk

How you can prevent the spread of non-native species

There are steps you can take to prevent non-native plants and animals spreading out of control.

Garden plants

When you are buying plants or seeds, or composting garden material, there are some precautions you can take to stop non-native species spreading:

⇨ try to use plants that are native to the UK;

⇨ always dispose of plant material or garden waste responsibly – don't dump it in the wild;

⇨ be careful with the plants you share with friends or move around.

You can find out about controlling non-native plants on the Department for Environment, Food and Rural Affairs (Defra) website (www.defra.gov.uk).

Pond plants

Pond and water plants can cause major problems when they get into lakes and rivers. It costs more than £3 million each year to control just three kinds of aquatic plants in Britain.

Animals or plants have been brought to this country for hundreds of years. Most of them are not a problem. However, some plants and animals spread more aggressively

Animals

There are many restrictions on bringing animals into the UK, and you will need a licence to bring in most non-native animals. The animal import laws help to protect crops and native wildlife, prevent diseases like rabies, and to stop the trade in endangered species.

Some animals are not allowed into the UK because of the danger to native wildlife. Other animals will need to be checked for disease before they can enter.

For more information on bringing plants and animals to the UK, download the leaflet on importing non-native plants and animals from the Natural England website (www.naturalengland.org.uk).

Releasing non-native animals into the wild

If you do import or keep an animal that is not native to the UK you must take care that it does not escape. You are responsible for the animal's welfare, and for making sure it is kept safely and securely.

If your animal does escape, or you release it into the wild, you can be prosecuted under the Wildlife and Countryside Act 1981.

In some cases you can get a licence to release non-native animals into the wild. For more information on licences to release non-native wildlife visit the Natural England website (www.naturalengland.org.uk).

⇨ The above information is reprinted with kind permission from Directgov. Visit www.direct.gov.uk for more information.

© Crown copyright

Wildlife crime unit

Information from the Metropolitan Police.

Exotic species in the wild

Over the years many species which do not normally live in the wild in Britain have been deliberately released here and many of these now have established populations in the wild. This can have a serious impact on our own wildlife as these animals are often more successful than similar species already living here, and a number of previously common British wild animals are now threatened by the presence of exotic species which compete with them for the habitat and food supplies in the area.

The grey squirrel, from North America, is probably the best known exotic species living in the London area, but there are many others including Muntjac deer from south-east Asia, red-eared terrapins and bullfrogs from the USA and ring-necked parakeets from India. In 2000, the Metropolitan Police and London Zoo even caught a lynx which was roaming free in North London.

Many of the terrapins and bullfrogs are examples of household pets which were deliberately released by their owners when they became too big or too difficult to look after. This is against the law, as in Britain it is an offence to deliberately release any species which does not normally live here.

How you can help

If you are thinking of buying an exotic pet make sure that you know as much as possible about how to care for it, how large it will grow, etc., before you buy. If you have an exotic pet which you are unable to keep any longer please contact a reputable animal welfare organisation like the RSPCA who may be able to help to re-home it. Remember, it is against the law to release it.

⇨ The above information is reprinted with kind permission from the Metropolitan Police. Visit www.met.police.uk for more information.

© Metropolitan Police

KEY FACTS

⇨ Tropical rainforests are the world's richest natural habitats, housing more than two-thirds of all plant and animal species on Earth. Sadly, the rainforests are being destroyed at an alarming rate – with more than half already gone. (page 1)

⇨ In 2004, researchers identified 146 dead zones around the world's coastlines, areas where the dissolved oxygen levels are so low that no marine life can be sustained. (page 2)

⇨ 95% of all animals and plants that have ever lived on Earth have now become extinct. (page 4)

⇨ We share the planet with as many as 13 million different living species including plants, animals and bacteria, only 1.75 million of which have been named and recorded. (page 6)

⇨ It is estimated that one-fifth of coral reefs are already seriously degraded or under imminent risk of collapse as a result of unsustainable human activities such as coastal developments, over-fishing, destructive fishing practices and pollution. (page 10)

⇨ The 'alarming' rate at which species are being lost could have a severe effect on humanity, conservationists warned today. Targets set eight years ago by governments to reduce biodiversity loss by 2010 have not been met. (page 13)

⇨ Land areas around the world totalling more than the size of Canada have been identified as having potential to be restored to good-quality, healthy forests, a new study has found. (page 15)

⇨ There is a growing body of scientific evidence on the adverse impacts of several man-made chemicals on wildlife species. Scientists have shown that many wildlife populations have already been affected by hormone disruptors. (page 16)

⇨ In the last century, elephant populations massively declined due to habitat destruction, increased agriculture and the ivory trade. Ivory poaching from 1979–89 halved Africa's elephant population from 1.3 million to 600,000. Today, numbers may be as low as 450,000. (page 19)

⇨ Countries across south-east Asia are being systematically drained of wildlife to meet a booming demand for exotic pets in Europe and Japan, and traditional medicine in China – posing a greater threat to many species than habitat loss or global warming. (page 20)

⇨ More than a quarter (27%) of European mammals have declining populations. (page 21)

⇨ Mankind's closest living relatives – the world's apes, monkeys, lemurs and other primates – are on the brink of extinction and in need of urgent conservation measures according to *Primates in Peril: The World's 25 Most Endangered Primates, 2008–2010*. (page 22)

⇨ At least 65% of all species on the planet are invertebrates. There are more than 32,000 terrestrial and freshwater and 7,000 marine species in the UK alone, and many are critically endangered. (page 26)

⇨ Pollinators – including honey and bumble bees, butterflies and moths – play an essential role in putting food on our tables through the pollination of many vital crops. However, the numbers of pollinators have been declining steadily in recent years, with the number of bees in the UK alone falling by between ten and 15 per cent over the last two years. (page 27)

⇨ A University of Aberdeen scientist has found that climate change is likely to affect where 88% of the world's whale, dolphin and porpoise species – collectively known as cetaceans – are found. (page 29)

⇨ The British taste for fish and chips could be driving species to the edge of extinction, according to a new survey that found the majority of people do not even try to make sustainable choices about seafood. (page 30)

⇨ 24% of butterflies, 22% of amphibians, 15% of dolphins and whales, 14% of stoneworts, 12% of terrestrial mammals and 12% of stoneflies have been lost from England. (page 31)

⇨ Lynx, brown bears, wolves and elk are among a range of animals being considered for reintroduction to the countryside centuries after they died out in Britain. (page 33)

⇨ Figures for butterfly sightings in 2009 have raised fears that five of Britain's rarest butterflies face a growing risk of extinction. (page 36)

Alien invasive species

These are species that, as a result of international trade including shipping or deliberate introductions, can flourish unchecked in their new homes, sometimes thousands of kilometres from where they are naturally found. This can damage ecosystems and native species.

Biodiversity

The variety of different life-forms which exist within a given area, or on the Earth in general. Its destruction can be damaging to complex ecosystems.

Bushmeat

Meat from wild animals. There is a thriving illegal trade in bushmeat.

Canned hunting

The hunting of wild animals in a confined area from which they cannot escape. The animals are hand-reared for the purpose and are often virtually tame. Hunters then pay a fee to shoot the animal at close range.

Climate change

Changes in the Earth's atmosphere can result in a rise in the overall temperature of the planet over a long period of time. This is also referred to as global warming.

Conservation

Safeguarding biodiversity; attempting to protect endangered species and their habitats from destruction.

Deforestation

The clearance of large areas of forest to obtain wood or land for cattle grazing.

Ecosystem

A system maintained by the interaction between different biological organisms within their physical environment, each one of which is important for the ecosystem to continue to function efficiently.

Endangered

A species which is at risk of becoming extinct is said to be endangered. The most commonly-used measure of how endangered a species has become is the IUCN Red List, which classifies endangered species as either Critically Endangered (CR), meaning that a species faces extremely high risk of extinction in the near future; Endangered (EN), meaning that a species faces a very high risk of extinction in the near future and Vulnerable (VU), meaning that a species is likely to become Endangered unless the circumstances threatening its survival and reproduction improve.

Endemic

Native or restricted to a particular place.

Extinct

If a species has become extinct, there are no surviving members of that species: it has died out completely.

Habitat

An area which supports certain conditions, allowing various species native to that area to live and thrive. When a species' 'natural habitat' is mentioned, this refers to the area it would usually occupy in the wild.

Invertebrate

Animal without a backbone.

Palm oil

Palm oil is the world's most popular vegetable oil. It is used in many products, including pizza, make-up and soap. Oil palm plantations are making a significant contribution to deforestation and ecosystem destruction.

Species

A specific type of living organism.

Vertebrate

Animal with a backbone.

access and benefit sharing of genetic resources 12

acidification of oceans 30

African elephants 2, 19

alien invasive species 12
  UK 38–9

Amazon forest destruction and cattle ranching 14

American bullfrogs, impact on UK wildlife 38

animals
  endangered *see* endangered species
  non-native, import restrictions 39
  reintroduction into Britain 33–4
  trade in exotic animals 20–21

Asian pangolins, trade in 21

bats, London 35

bears, reintroduction into Britain 33–4

beavers, reintroduction into Britain 34

bees, declining numbers 27–8

bioaccumulative chemicals 16

biodiversity
  and global economy 10–12
  importance of 6
  key scientific questions 7
  and oil palm industry 8–9

biodiversity loss 13
  England 31–2

black redstarts, London 35

Brazil, cattle ranching and deforestation 14

Britain *see* United Kingdom

bushmeat trade 23

butterflies, Britain 36

canned hunting 17

carbon dioxide level increase, effect on oceans 30

cattle ranching and rainforest destruction 14

caviar, illegal trade 4

chemicals, impact on wildlife 16–17

CITES (The Convention on International Trade in Endangered Species) 2

climate change 5
  effect on Galápagos Islands 24–5
  impact on whales and dolphins 29

CO_2 level increase, effect on oceans 30

Congo, logging industry 4

Congo river 4

consumption, humans 3–4

cooperation, international 12

coral reefs 5
  economic value 10

costs, alien invasive species 12

deforestation
  and cattle ranching 14
  and palm oil industry 8–9

dolphins, impact of climate change 29

economic role of biodiversity 10–12

EDCs (endocrine disrupting chemicals) 16–17

elephants 2, 19

empty forest syndrome 20

endangered species 1–2
  butterflies 36
  elephants 19
  fish 30
  invertebrates 26
  pollinating insects 27–8
  primates 22–3
  tigers 18
  UK 31–2, 35, 36
  whales and dolphins 29

endocrine disrupting chemicals (EDCs) 16–17

England, loss of biodiversity 31–2

environmental governance, international 12

exotic pets 20–21, 39

exotic species in the wild, Britain 39

fish 30

floating pennywort 38

forests 4
  empty forest syndrome 20
  rainforest destruction 1, 5
  restoration 15
  see also deforestation

freshwater resources 5

frogs and toads, London 35

Galápagos Islands 24–5

geckos, trade in 21

genetic resources, sharing 12

Global Partnership on Forest Restoration (GPFLR) 15

grey squirrels, effects of 38

habitat destruction 1
  see also deforestation

hedgehogs, London 35

hormone disrupting chemicals 16–17

house sparrows, London 35

humans, effect on earth's resources 3–5

hunting 1–2
  for bushmeat trade 23
  of captive animals 17

Indonesia, palm oil industry 8–9

inequality of resource usage 4

insects 26
  pollinating, declining numbers 27–8
  stag beetles, London 35

Intergovernmental Panel on Biodiversity and Ecosystem Services (IPBES) 10–11

international environment governance 12

invertebrates 26

IPBES (Intergovernmental Panel on Biodiversity and Ecosystem Services) 10–11

ivory trade 2, 19

Japanese knotweed 38

logging, effect on wildlife 4
London, rare species 35
lynx, reintroduction into Britain 33, 34

meat, wild animals hunted for meat 23

non-native species, impact of 12
  UK 38–9

ocean acidification 30

palm oil industry 8–9
pangolins, trade in 21
peregrine falcons, London 35
persistent chemicals 16
pets, exotic 20–21, 39
phytoplankton 5
pollinating insects, declining numbers 27–8
pollution 2
porpoises, impact of climate change 29
primates 22–3

rainforest destruction 1, 5
red squirrels, Scotland 37
reintroduction of animals into Britain 33–4
rhinos 1–2
Roundtable on Sustainable Palm Oil (RSPO) 9

Scotland
  red squirrels 37
  reintroduction of animals 33–4
seahorses, trade in 21
sparrows, London 35
species loss 13
  England 31–2
  Galápagos Islands 24–5
species reintroduction, Britain 33–4

squirrels
  grey 38
  red 37
stag beetles, London 35

tigers 1, 18
timber industry 4
tokay geckos, trade in 21
trade
  caviar 4
  exotic animals, Asia 20–21
  ivory 19
trapping 1
tropical rainforest destruction 1, 5

United Kingdom 31–9
  bee and pollinator decline 27–8
  biodiversity loss 31–2
  butterfly numbers declining 36
  non-native wildlife 38–9
  red squirrels, Scotland 37
  reintroduction of animals 33–4
  threatened species in London 35
United Nations Environment Programme (UNEP) 10–11, 13
USA, environmental impact 5

water voles, London 35
whales
  hunted 1
  impact of climate change 29
wildlife
  impact of chemicals 16–17
  impact of non-native species 12, 38–9
  London 35
  reintroduction of species into Britain 33-4
wolves, reintroduction into Britain 33, 34

ZSL, Biodiversity and Oil Palm project 8–9

Additional Resources

Other Issues titles

If you are interested in researching further some of the issues raised in *Endangered Species,* you may like to read the following titles in the **Issues** series:

⇨ Vol. 161 *Waste Issues* (ISBN 978 1 86168 454 7)

⇨ Vol. 157 *The Problem of Globalisation* (ISBN 978 1 86168 444 8)

⇨ Vol. 151 *Climate Change* (ISBN 978 1 86168 424 0)

⇨ Vol. 146 *Sustainability and Environment* (ISBN 978 1 86168 419 6)

⇨ Vol. 97 *Energy Matters* (ISBN 978 1 86168 305 2)

For a complete list of available **Issues** titles, please visit our website: www.independence.co.uk/shop

Useful organisations

You may find the websites of the following organisations useful for further research:

⇨ **Animal Aid:** www.animalaid.org.uk

⇨ **David Shepherd Wildlife Foundation:** www.davidshepherd.org

⇨ **IYB-UK:** www.biodiversityislife.net

⇨ **Natural Environment Research Council:** www.nerc.ac.uk

⇨ **UN Environment Programme:** www.unep.org

ACKNOWLEDGEMENTS

The publisher is grateful for permission to reproduce the following material.

While every care has been taken to trace and acknowledge copyright, the publisher tenders its apology for any accidental infringement or where copyright has proved untraceable. The publisher would be pleased to come to a suitable arrangement in any such case with the rightful owner.

Chapter One: The International Situation

Endangered species, © Animal Aid, *Shocking global facts,* © David Shepherd Wildlife Foundation, *Detailed status of UK Priority Species in 2008 [graph],* © Crown copyright is reproduced with the permission of Her Majesty's Stationery Office, *Why does biodiversity matter to me?,* © CBD-UN International Year of Biodiversity www.biodiversityislife.net, *100 questions to conserve global biodiversity,* © Natural Environment Research Council, *Biodiversity and Oil Palm project,* © ZSL, *Number of threatened vertebrate species by year and taxonomic group [graph],* © IUCN, *Boosting biodiversity can boost global economy,* © United Nations Environment Programme, *Threatened species in each region [graph],* © IUCN, *UN report warns of economic impact of biodiversity loss,* © Guardian News and Media Limited 2010, *Brazil cattle giants unite to end Amazon destruction,* © Greenpeace, *Billion hectares of land have potential for forest restoration, study shows,* © Forestry Commission, *Wildlife – cause for concern,* © CHEM Trust, *Canned hunting,* © Born Free Foundation, *Year of the tiger,* © WWF-UK, *Elephants under threat,* © Born Free Foundation, *How the pet trade's greed is emptying south-east Asia's forests,* © Guardian News and Media Limited 2010, *European Red List: summary of key findings [graphs],* © European Commission, *World's most endangered primates revealed,* © Bristol Zoo, IUCN and Conservation International, *What is the bushmeat trade?,* © Born Free Foundation, *Galápagos,* © Conservation International, *Numbers of Critically Endangered and Extinct mammal, bird and amphibian species occurring in and endemic to each of the 34 individual hotspots [table],* © Conservation International, *Why we need to conserve invertebrates,* © Buglife, *£10m initiative to tackle bee and pollinator decline,* © Natural Environment Research Council, *Number of threatened invertebrate species by year and taxonomic group [graph],* © IUCN, *Whales and dolphins in hot water,* © University of Aberdeen, *Ocean acidification,* © The NHSM/IYB-UK www.biodiversityislife.net, *Consumer ignorance over endangered fish,* © Telegraph Media Group Limited 2010.

Chapter Two: The UK Situation

Lost life: England's lost and threatened species, © Natural England 2010, *Bears, lynx, wolves and elk considered for reintroduction to British countryside,* © Telegraph Media Group Limited 2010, *Detailed status of UK Priority Habitats in 2008 [graph],* © Crown copyright is reproduced with the permission of Her Majesty's Stationery Office, *London's priority species,* © London Wildlife Trust, *Fears grow for future of Britain's rarest butterflies,* © Butterfly Conservation, *Red squirrel threats,* © Scottish Wildlife Trust, *Controlling non-native wildlife,* © Crown copyright is reproduced with the permission of Her Majesty's Stationery Office, *Wildlife crime unit,* © Metropolitan Police.

Illustrations

Pages 1, 14, 20, 28: Don Hatcher; pages 3, 19, 32, 35: Angelo Madrid; pages 6, 16, 22, 33: Simon Kneebone; pages 8, 18: Bev Aisbett.

Cover photography

Left: © René te Witt. Centre: © Philip MacKenzie. Right: © Thiago Floriano.

Additional acknowledgements

Research by Sabrine Paupiah.

Additional research by Hart McLeod Limited, Cambridge.

And with thanks to the Independence team: Mary Chapman, Sandra Dennis and Jan Sunderland.

Lisa Firth
Cambridge
May, 2010